SOUTHERN

LADIES

KNOW HOW TO COOK IT

copyright 1998
Library of Congress Catalog #98-96735
Sharon A. Strickland
Rosemary A. Newman
Cover Photograph: Joseph Byrd
Design: Georgia R. Byrd

About the Authors

We grew up in the mountains of North Carolina not far from the Great Smoky Mountains. Our mother and grandmother were two typical mountain women that could take anything on hand, and when finished, we knew we were in for a treat. We remember many days when supper was scratching at the ground at breakfast, and on a platter on the table for supper.

As years went by we left our home in our beloved mountains. Both moved to coastal areas (Sharon to South Carolina, Rose to Savannah, Georgia). In between, we left most of our families and a lot of good cooks.

We have taken a combination of poetry, mountain and Southern remedies, and everyone's best recipes from the mountains to the coast, and have incorporated them into the very best of the best Southern cooking.

We thank you for the honor of becoming part of your cooking library. We hope as you try these recipes, you will agree, "Southern Ladies Know How to Cook It!"

Mama's Garden

While planting my garden on a warm spring day,
my mind wasn't on it, it was far away.
To a day filled with sunshine much like this,
soft breezes blowing with a warm gentle kiss.
To another garden with two people standing arm in arm,
admiring the beauty, doing no harm.
Talking of summer and what it would bring,
hearts beating with joy as the birds sing.
Alone in the garden they pass the hours,
discussing the beauty of the flowers.
But time goes on and seasons pass,
I still can't think of anything as sweet as a day in her garden
just Mama and me, feeling everything's right,
just the way it should be.
My mind returns to the present, my planting is done
It's just me now, Mama is gone.
But she'll always be with me in my mind,
each time I see a flower I'm sure I'll find.
The beauty of her laughter, the brilliance of her smile,
So I'll nurture my garden and we'll visit awhile.

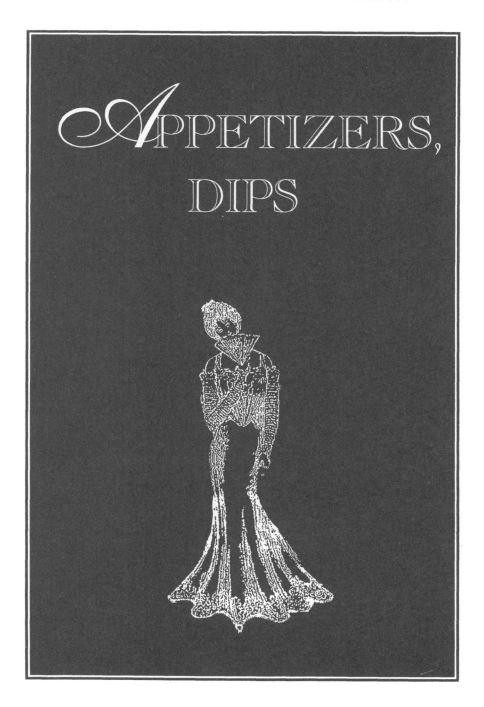

APPETIZERS, DIPS

CREAM CHEESE PINEAPPLE SANDWICHES

2 8 oz. Packages cream cheese
1 20 oz. Can crushed pineapple, drained
1 Cup chopped pecans
1 Cup powdered sugar
2 Loaves white bread
1 Loaf grain bread
Few drops of green food coloring

Cream cheese and sugar together until light and fluffy. Add pineapple and pecans; mix well. Divide mixture in half; add a few drops of food coloring until desired shade is reached in half of the mixture. Remove crust from breads. Spread some of the uncolored mixture on top of a slice of white bread. Top with a slice of grain bread; spread some of the colored mixture on top of grain bread; top with slice of white bread. Cut into quarters. Repeat until all is used.

CHICKEN SALAD BALLS

2 Cup finely chopped cooked chicken
2 Tablespoons grated onion
1/2 Teaspoon hot sauce, optional
1/2 Cup mayonnaise
1/4 Cup pimentos, chopped
1-2 Cups chopped pecans

Mix ingredients in order listed, except pecans; mix well. Dip mixture out by rounded teaspoons and roll into balls. Chill for about 1/2 hour. Roll in chopped pecans to coat.

SAUCY DOGS

1 1/2 Pounds beef hot dogs
1 Can tomato soup
2 Tablespoons margarine
1 Teaspoon mustard
1/3 Cup chopped green pepper
1/3 Cup chopped onion
4 Teaspoons Worcestershire sauce

Cut the hot dogs into bite-size pieces. Saute pepper and onion in margarine in a heavy saucepan. When tender, add remaining ingredients along with the hot dogs. Reduce heat and simmer for 10 minutes.

PIMENTO CHEESE SPREAD

1 Pound sharp Cheddar cheese
3/4 Cup mayonnaise
Salt to taste
1 Jar pimentos, drained

Grate cheese. Add pimentos and mayonnaise. Mix well. Better if made the day before in order for flavors to blend. Store in airtight container in refrigerator.

OLIVE NUGGETS

8 oz. Sharp Cheddar cheese
1 Stick margarine,
1/4 Teaspoon salt
1 1/2 Cups sifted flour
1 Teaspoon onion powder
45-50 Medium stuffed olives

Shred cheese and cream with margarine. Combine
salt, flour and onion powder. Mix into cheese mixture to
form a soft dough. Pinch off enough of dough to mold
around each olive. Place on ungreased cookie sheet and
bake at 400 degrees for 10-12 minutes or until golden
brown. If desired, cut recipe in half for a small gathering

BAR-B-QUED SMOKED SAUSAGE

1 1/2 Pounds smoked sausage
1 1/2 Cups dark brown sugar
1 1/2 Cups ketchup
1/4 Cup Worcestershire sauce
2 Tablespoons prepared mustard

Cut sausage into bite-size pieces. Fry until done and
brown. Combine sugar, ketchup, Worcestershire sauce
and mustard in a saucepan. Add sausage and cook on
medium heat until boiling point is reached. Pour into a
chafing dish to serve.

CHEESE PENNIES

2 Sticks margarine, softened
1 Package dry onion soup mix
8 oz. American cheese
2 Cups flour

Combine ingredients; mix well. Divide mixture and roll each half into the shape of a log. Refrigerate until chilled. Cut into 1/4-inch slices. Place on ungreased cookie sheet and bake at 375 degrees for 10 minutes.

SKEDADDLE AH, NUTS

3oz can Chinese noodles
1/2 Cup evaporated milk
1 Cup miniature marshmallows
1 Cup roasted peanuts
3/4 Cup sugar
2 Tablespoons butter
1 6 oz. Package chocolate morsels

Combine Chinese noodles, marshmallows and peanuts and set aside. In a heavy saucepan, bring sugar, milk and butter to a full boil, stirring constantly until sugar melts. Remove from heat and stir in chocolate until melted. Allow to stand for 15 minutes. Stir mixture and pour over noodle mixture; stir until well coated. Drop by rounded teaspoons onto waxed paper-lined cookie sheet. Chill until set. Remove from paper.

FRESH FRUIT PLATTER

1 Whole pineapple
Kiwi fruit
Star fruit
Pears
Oranges
Red delicious apples
Golden delicious apples
Red and white grapes
Fresh strawberries with caps

Leave cap on pineapple and slice lengthwise. Cut out insides without damaging shell. Slice pineapple into cubes and discard core. Place shell in middle of large platter. Wash and dry fruit. Slice kiwi, star fruit, pears, oranges and both kinds of apples. Leave grapes and strawberries whole. Arrange them around the pineapple shell. Pour fruit into shell just before serving.

Fruit dressing:
2 3oz. Packages cream cheese
2 Tablespoons lemon juice
3 Tablespoons sugar
1 1/2 Cups whipping cream

Blend first three ingredients. Beat whipping cream. Stir into blended mixture. Chill until ready to use. This makes about 3 cups.

VEGETABLE DIP

1 Cup salad dressing
1 1/2 Tablespoons grated onion
1 Tablespoon chopped celery
1 Tablespoon lemon juice
1 Tablespoon Worcestershire sauce
1/2 Teaspoon garlic salt

Combine ingredients; mix well. To save time, make ahead and store in refrigerator.

CRAB DIP

2 Cans white crab meat
2 Teaspoons horseradish
6 Tablespoons French dressing
1/2 Cup finely grated Cheddar cheese

Combine ingredients; mix well. Serve with a variety of crackers.

SHRIMP DIP

2 3oz. Package cream cheese, softened
2 Cups sour cream
1 Tablespoon lemon juice
2 Packages dry Italian dressing mix
1 Cup finely chopped cooked shrimp

Cream the cheese; add other ingredients in order listed. Mix well. Serve with assorted crackers.

CRAB CHEDDAR POUCHES

1 Can flaky refrigerator biscuits
1-7 1/2 oz. Can crab meat, drained and flaked
1/2 Cup mayonnaise
1 Tablespoon grated onion
1 Teaspoon lemon juice
Pinch of curry powder
4 oz. Cheddar cheese, shredded

Combine crab meat, mayonnaise, onion, lemon juice, curry powder and cheese; mix thoroughly. Separate biscuits into three layers. Place about 3/4 of a teaspoon of mixture in center of each layer of biscuits. Bring layers up on all sides to make a pouch. Pinch top of pouch together to seal. Bake at 400 degrees for 10-12 minutes or until golden brown.

CHEDDAR CHEESE PUFFS

1 Cup grated cheddar cheese
1/2 Cup margarine
1 1/2 Cups sifted flour
1/4 Teaspoon salt
1/2 tsp. Cayenne pepper, more or less

Cream the cheese and margarine until smooth. Add flour, salt and pepper. Knead just until soft dough forms. Take small pieces and roll into balls. Place on greased cookie sheet and bake at 400 degrees 10-12 minutes or until nicely browned.

ITALIAN DIP

8 oz. Cream cheese
1 Jar pizza sauce
1 Pound Italian sausage
1 Small onion, chopped
1 Small bell pepper, chopped
2 Cups cheese, Cheddar and Mozzarella
1 Can black olives, drained

Crumble sausage and fry until completely done. Layer ingredients in order listed into baking dish. Bake at 375 degrees for 25-30 minutes or until cheese is brown and bubbly. Serve with large scoop-size corn chips.

PARMESAN STUFFED MUSHROOMS

24 Medium mushrooms
4 Tablespoons chopped onion
1/8 Teaspoon chopped garlic
4 Tablespoons butter
1/2 Teaspoon parsley flakes
Salt and pepper to taste
1/2 Cup Parmesan cheese

Cut end off mushroom stem and discard. Remove stems from caps and chop fine. In a skillet, melt butter; add chopped stems, onion and garlic. Saute for 5 minutes or until tender. Combine all ingredients, except mushroom caps, and remove from heat right away. Fill caps with mixture and place on greased baking sheet. Bake at 350 degrees for 15-17 minutes.

DEVILED HAM DIP

2-2 1/4 oz. Cans deviled ham
1/2 Cup sour cream
1/4 Cup mayonnaise
1/2 Teaspoon paprika
3 Tablespoons chopped green onions
1 1/4 Teaspoons Worcestershire sauce

Combine ingredients; mix well. Sprinkle additional paprika over dip if desired. Place in bowl on serving tray along with a variety of crackers.

STRAWBERRY DIP

1 8oz. Package cream cheese
1 6-oz. Jar marshmallow creme
1/2 Teaspoon butternut vanilla flavoring

Cream the cheese and marshmallow cream until light and fluffy. Add butternut-vanilla flavoring; continue to beat a few more seconds. Place in a decorative bowl on a platter and surround with cleaned, fresh strawberries with caps on.

* Helpful hint: If strawberries aren't going to be used right away, store in refrigerator unwashed for longer shelf life.

CHEESE DUMPLIN'S IN TOMATO SAUCE

1 Can tomato soup
1 Cup water
Salt and pepper to taste
1 Tablespoon grated onion
2 Cups boxed biscuit mix
1 Cup cheese, grated
3/4 Cup milk

Bring to a boil soup and water that seasonings have been added to. Combine other ingredients to make a soft dough. Drop from a teaspoon into boiling soup. Cover and reduce heat. Cook for 20 minutes. Do not uncover while cooking.

CHEESE SOUFFLE

3 Tablespoons butter
3 Tablespoons flour
1 Cup milk
3 Egg yolks
1/2 Teaspoon salt
1 Cup grated cheese
3 Egg whites

Melt butter, stir in flour, then add milk and stir until thickened. Stir in a little of hot mixture into yolks, then add to rest of hot mixture along with the cheese and salt. Beat egg whites until stiff but not dry and fold into cheese mixture. Pour into baking dish that has been sprayed with non-stick spray. Set in pan of hot water and bake at 300 degrees for 35 minutes. Serve right away.

Soups & Salads

⨍ SOUTHERN LADIES ⨍
KNOW HOW TO COOK IT!

DELICIOUS
CREATIONS!

God's Garden

As you walk out in the world
each and every day,
think of all your blessings God
has sent your way.
Bend and pick a flower and
notice carefully,
how each little leaf and petal
are shaped so perfectly.
Think of the hand that places
them there with such loving care,
and I know you will surely feel
The Almighty's presence there.
It's through His love and kindness
He sews His garden carefully,
and gives so in abundance blessings
to you and me.
So when you have a bad day and
life seems so unfair,
take a walk in God's garden
He's always glad to share.

Copyright 1997
Sharon A. Strickland

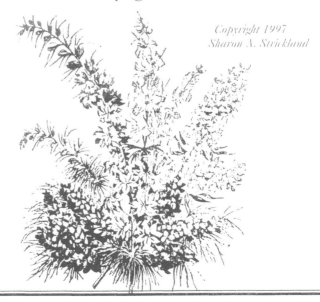

14

MACARONI SALAD

1 12-oz. Package macaroni
1/2 Cup Vidalia onions, chopped
1/2 Cup chopped celery
1 Small jar pimentos
Salt and pepper to taste
1 Cup mayonnaise
1 Tablespoon lemon juice
1/2 Large green pepper chopped
1/2 Cup raisins

Cook macaroni according to package directions. Drain and allow cool. While still slightly warm, add rest of ingredients. Refrigerate in airtight container. Better if made the day before.

KILLED LETTUCE AND ONIONS

1 Large head of lettuce
1 Cup chopped green onions, including blades
Hot fat-back grease

Shred lettuce, add onions and toss. Pour hot fat-back grease over, and toss again. Very good with buttermilk and cornbread.

This is one of our absolute favorites from childhood. Sissy would go out and pick greens from the side of a branch. She called this branch lettuce. We don't know how this salad got its name, unless it's because when the hot grease is poured on, it wilts the lettuce and onions.

CHICKEN SALAD

3 Cups chopped chicken
1/2 Cups chopped celery
2 Hard boiled eggs, chopped
1/2 Cup sweet pickle cubes
1/3 Cup Miracle Whip
Salt to taste

Mix ingredients together. Store in airtight container in refrigerator. Better if made the day before.

TYBEE ISLAND SHRIMP SALAD

1 1/2-3 lbs.. Medium shrimp
1/3 Cup celery, finely chopped
1/4 Cup sweet pickle relish
3/4 Cup mayonnaise
1 Pack ranch dressing
2 Hard boiled eggs

Bring water and salt to full boil. Add shrimp and boil until done (about 5-6 minutes). Drain and cool. When cooled, peel and coarsely chop. Combine celery, relish, and mayonnaise, stirring well. To this, add ranch dressing and mix thoroughly. Gently stir in eggs.

This makes a pretty luncheon dish served on leaf lettuce with a tomato and pickle wedge. Also great for a sandwich on toasted bread.

Helpful Hint: When recipe calls for shrimp, they should be weighed after heads are removed.

"If you wake with a light heart,
Sing!"— Rosemary Newman

SOUTHERN LADIES
KNOW HOW TO COOK IT!

SALAD
FIXINS'

CUCUMBER SALAD

1 Package lime gelatin
3/4 Cup boiling water
1/4 Cup lemon juice
1 Teaspoon liquid onion
1 Cup sour cream
1 Cup finely chopped cucumbers
1/4 Cup mayonnaise

Dissolve gelatin in boiling water. Stir in lemon and onion juice. Chill until slightly set. Combine rest of ingredients and stir into gelatin. Pour into mold and chill until firm.

CAULIFLOWER SALAD

1 Large head cauliflower
2 Cups mayonnaise
1 Tablespoon white vinegar
1/2 Cup finely chopped green onion or Vidalia
1 Tablespoon sugar
10-oz. Package frozen small green peas, thawed
1/2 Cup shredded cheese
1/2 Cup chopped pecans
1 Small jar pimentos, chopped

Cut cauliflower into bite-size pieces. Place in salad bowl and layer onion, peas and cheese on top of cauliflower. Combine mayonnaise, vinegar, sugar, pecans and pimentos; mix well. Pour over salad and refrigerate. Best if made the day before.

CRANBERRY SALAD

1 Pound cranberries
2 Large Rome apples
Juice and rind of orange
3/4 Cup chopped celery
2 Cups + 2 tablespoons sugar
3 Packages lemon gelatin
1 Small can crushed pineapple, drained
3/4 Cup chopped celery
1 Cup chopped walnuts
3 Cups boiling water

Grind cranberries and apples together. Add orange juice, rind and sugar. Place in refrigerator for 2-3 hours to allow flavors to blend. Dissolve gelatin in water and allow to cool. Add rest of ingredients into cranberry mixture. Stir into gelatin and refrigerate until firm.

PINEAPPLE CHEESE SALAD

1 Package lime gelatin
1 Cup boiling water
1 Small can crushed pineapple, drained
1 Small can milk evaporated
1 Cup grated cheese
1/2 Cup mayonnaise

Dissolve gelatin in water. Allow to cool. Add rest of ingredients into gelatin. Chill until firm.

"Mama's garden was always full of
fresh vegetables!"

SOUTHERN LADIES
KNOW HOW TO COOK IT!

COOKING IS
FUN!

AMBROSIA

2 Medium bananas sliced
3/4 Cup chopped orange
1 Cup frozen coconut, thawed
1 Cup red seedless grapes
1 1/2 Cup pineapple tidbits
1 Cup miniature marshmallows
1 Carton sour cream
2 Tablespoons sugar

Stir sugar into cream; set aside. Combine other ingredients in order; mix well. Stir in sour cream mixture. Refrigerate overnight for flavors to blend.

WALDORF SALAD

2 Cups red apples, unpeeled
1 Cup chopped celery
1/2 Cup pecans
1/2 Cup white raisins
1/2 - 3/4 Cup salad dressing

Wash and core apples; cut into cubes. Combine ingredients in a large bowl; mix well. Chill several hours before serving.

EASY HAM SALAD

1 1/2 Cups ground ham
5 Hard-boiled eggs
1/2 Jar sandwich spread

Combine ingredients and mix thoroughly. Refrigerate in airtight container.

TUNA SALAD

1 6-1/2 oz. Can tuna, drained
2 Hard-boiled eggs
3 Heaping tablespoons mayonnaise
2 Tablespoons sweet pickle relish
1/2 Teaspoon salt
1/2 Teaspoon pepper

Combine ingredients. Store in airtight container in refrigerator. Better if made the day before use.

EGG SALAD

6 Large hard-boiled eggs
3 Heaping Tablespoons mayonnaise
2 Heaping tablespoons sweet pickle relish
Salt and pepper to taste

Mix ingredients thoroughly. Refrigerate in airtight container. Better if made the day before use.

HEAVENLY HASH

2 Cups thawed whipped topping
3 Tablespoons milk
1 Can crushed pineapple drained well
1 Cup frozen coconut thawed
1/2 Cup chopped maraschino cherries
1 Cup miniature marshmallows
1/2 Cup chopped pecans, optional

Mix ingredients, stirring well. Refrigerate several hours before serving.

CARROT AND RAISIN SALAD

2 Cups grated carrots
1/2 Can pineapple tidbits, drained well
1 Cup raisins
2 Tablespoons orange juice
3/4 Cup salad dressing
2 Tablespoons sugar

Combine all, mix well. Cover and chill for several hours before serving. Good made the day before.

MAMA'S POTATO SALAD

5-6 Potatoes
8 Hard-boiled eggs
1 Teaspoon salt
1 Medium onion, chopped
1/2 Small jar sweet pickle cubes
1/2 - 3/4 Cup mayonnaise
Paprika for garnish

Peel and dice potatoes. Place in large saucepan, cover with cold water, add salt, cover and boil until tender. Drain. Chop 6 of the hard-boiled eggs and add to hot potatoes along with the onion, pickles and mayonnaise. Mix well. Spoon into bowl and garnish with last 2 eggs that have been sliced, and paprika. Good hot or cold.

SHARON'S POTATO SALAD

5-6 Potatoes
6 Hard-boiled eggs
1 Teaspoon salt
1 Medium onion, chopped
1/2 Small jar hot dog relish
1/4-1/2 Cup mayonnaise
Paprika for garnish

Peel and dice potatoes. In a large saucepan, cover potatoes with cold water, add salt and boil. Cook until tender. Drain. Chop eggs and add to hot potatoes, along with the onion, relish and mayonnaise. Mix well. Spoon into bowl. Smooth top and garnish with paprika. Cover and refrigerate.

BROCCOLI CHEDDAR SOUP

4 Tablespoons butter
6 Tablespoons flour
2 Cups heavy cream
2 Cups chicken stock
1 Cup evaporated milk
1 Cup water
Salt and pepper to taste
1 Package frozen broccoli, thawed
2 Cups Cheddar cheese

Melt margarine and add flour, salt and pepper (best to use white pepper), stirring to make a smooth paste. Do not brown. Add stock, milk and water, blending well. Add broccoli and cheese, heating thoroughly.

MINUTE STEAK STEW

1 Pound cubed steak
Flour for rolling
1/2 Cup oil
1 Onion, chopped
Salt and pepper to taste
1 Large can tomato sauce
3 Potatoes diced
1 Small can carrots
1 Small can peas

Cut steak in 1-inch cubes. Combine flour, salt and pepper. Roll steak in flour mixture. Brown steak on both sides in heated oil. Add onion and cook until tender. Pour off excess oil. Add remaining ingredients and simmer for 20-25 minutes or until potatoes are tender.

CREAM OF TOMATO SOUP

2 Cups tomatoes
2 Slices onion
3/4 Teaspoon salt
1/4 Cup flour
1/4 Cup butter
2 Cups milk

Simmer tomatoes and onion covered for 15 minutes. Strain and discard pulp. Return juice to pot and heat. Add flour and butter to tomato juice until thickened. Add milk slowly to juice, stirring constantly. Heat almost to boiling (do not boil). Serve immediately.

CORN CHOWDER

2 Cups creamed corn
1 Cup diced tomatoes
1 Cup V-8 Juice
1 Cup celery diced
4 Cups water
3 Tablespoons margarine
3 Tablespoons chopped pimentos
Salt to taste
1/3 Cup water
3 Tablespoons flour
3/4 Cup Cheddar cheese
Pinch of soda
1 Cup evaporated milk

In a large pot combine first 5 ingredients and cook until celery is tender. Add the next 5 ingredients in order and bring to a boil. Combine soda and milk and add to hot mixture. Heat thoroughly. Serve immediately. Sprinkle cheese on top.

BRUNSWICK STEW

2 Pounds pork, cubed
2 Pounds beef, cubed
1 Large can tomatoes
1 16-oz. Can creamed corn
1 Small can whole-kernel corn
4 Tablespoons Worcestershire
   sauce

2 Tablespoons white
   vinegar
1/3 Cup light brown su
   or molasses
8 Strips Bacon, fried
   and crumbled

Boil pork and beef until tender (venison may be substituted for beef). Reserve 2 cups of stock the meat was cooked in. Grind both meats in a food processor or blender. In a large pot, combine stock and all ingredients except creamed corn and bacon. Cover and cook on low heat for about 1 hour. Add creamed corn and bacon the last half hour. You may like to add more or less brown sugar, and more stock. We like ours kind of sweet and thick.

VEGETABLE BEEF SOUP

1 1/2 Pounds ground beef
1 Large can tomatoes
1 8oz. Bottle V-8 Juice
2 Large potatoes, diced
1 Large onion, diced
1 Can whole-kernel corn
1 16oz Can green beans
1 16oz. Can carrots
1 16oz. Can field peas
1 Cup sliced okra
1 16oz. Can garden peas
2 Tablespoons bacon fat

Fry ground beef until completely done; drain. Combine ingredients in order listed in a large pot. Cover and bring to boil on high. Reduce to low and cook for 45 minutes to 1 hour. Stir occasionally.

VEGETABLES

"If you're looking for someone to come, it is said, "a watched pot never boils."

A Gardener's Life

I didn't hear the clock alarm!
I've overslept, OH SHUCKS!
Here it is 6:30 and the sun is coming up!
So in a hurry off I go, the coffee pot
is waiting.
Then off to shower and brush my teeth
without any hesitating.
Back through the house I go,
I grab my favorite cup.
Get a burst of energy with every single gulp.
Then out the door to the shed,
I arm myself with shovel, hoe
and spade.
Pull on the boots, yank on the gloves,
as through a jungle of weeds I wade.
Faster, faster, still I go, get that weed chop, chop.
Pull out my trusty handkerchief and from my brow
the sweat I mop.
Now wait a minute, could it be?
Is that my alarm clock calling me?
Yes indeed! It's time to get up!
But I'm still tired it seems,
I feel as if I worked all night, maybe in my dreams?
So in a hurry off I go the coffee pot is waiting
Then off to shower and brush my teeth without any hesitating.
I finish up my morning routine,
and as I head on out the door,
I get an uneasy feeling
I've done all this before.

ONION RINGS

1 Large onion
1 3/4 Cup flour
1/4 Cup cornmeal
1/2 Teaspoon salt
2 Eggs
1 Cup buttermilk
Oil for deep frying

Slice onion, separate rings and set aside. Combine ingredients in order listed. Mix well. In a deep fryer or heavy pot, heat oil until hot. Dip each ring in batter and place immediately into hot oil. Fry until golden brown. Remove and drain on paper towels. Salt and serve while hot.

BATTERED FRENCH FRIES

2-3 Large potatoes
2 Cups flour
1/2 Teaspoon salt
1/4 Teaspoon pepper
2 Eggs
1 Cup buttermilk
Oil for deep frying

Scrub potatoes leaving skins on, slice french fry style. Set aside. Combine rest of ingredients to make a batter. Heat oil in a deep fryer or heavy pot until hot. Dip each potato slice into the batter and drop into hot oil. Fry until golden brown, remove and drain on paper towels. Salt and serve right away. Sweet potatoes can also be prepared this way. Replace pepper with 3/4 teaspoon cinnamon

FRIED SQUASH

6 Medium crooked neck squash
1 Cup self-rising cornmeal
1/2 Cup self-rising flour
Salt and pepper to taste
Vegetable oil for frying

Mix cornmeal, flour, salt, and pepper. Clean and slice squash into 1/4-inch slices. Roll in cornmeal mixture and fry in hot oil. Brown on both sides. Drain on paper towels. Serve hot.

SQUASH CASSEROLE

3 Cups cooked squash
1 Small onion, chopped
2 Eggs, slightly beaten
1/2 Cup milk
1 Cup Ritz crackers, crushed
1 Tablespoon margarine
Salt and pepper to taste
1 Tablespoon sugar
1 1/2 Cup Cheddar cheese, grated

Combine ingredients and mix well. Pour into large casserole that has been sprayed with non-stick spray. Bake in 350-degree oven for 30-35 minutes. Sprinkle with crushed potato chips, if desired, for the last 10 minutes of baking.

CHEESY POTATOES

4 Tablespoons butter
4 Tablespoons flour
1 Cup evaporated milk
1 Cup water from potatoes
Salt to taste
1 Cup grated Cheddar cheese
4 Cups diced potatoes

Cook potatoes just until tender. Drain, reserving 1 cup of liquid. Melt butter; add flour and salt, stir until smooth, but not brown. Add milk and liquid from potatoes; stir until thickened. Add cheese and cook until melted, stirring constantly. Place potatoes in a greased casserole dish and pour cheese mixture over and stir. Bake in a 350 degree oven for 35-40 minutes. Sauce should be bubbly and brown.

FRESH FRIED CORN

8 Ears fresh corn
3 Tablespoons cold bacon fat
2-3 Tablespoons sugar
Salt and pepper to taste

Cut kernels from cob into a bowl. Stir in sugar and seasonings. Pour into frying pan with cold bacon grease. Cover and cook on medium until tender. Stir frequently to prevent scorching. Cook until corn is tender.

BROCCOLI CASSEROLE

1 Package frozen broccoli, thawed
2 Eggs, beaten
1 Can cream of mushroom soup
1 Cup mayonnaise
1 Cup shredded Cheddar Cheese

Combine ingredients in order, mixing well. Pour into greased deep casserole dish. Bake at 400 degrees for 40-45 minutes or until golden brown. Can be made the day before.Good hot or cold.

MAMA'S NEW FRIED POTATOES

6-8 New red potatoes
Salt and pepper to taste
Butter or margarine for frying

Wash and scrape potatoes. In a medium saucepan, cover with cold water. Bring to boil on high heat. Reduce to medium and continue to cook until done but firm. Don't overcook. Gently remove potatoes from water and drain on paper towels. Melt butter or margarine in heavy frying pan. Slice potatoes lengthwise down middle. Salt and pepper, if desired. Brown on both sides. Drain on paper towels. Serve hot.

PICKLED BEETS

6 medium beets
1/2 Cup vinegar
1 Teaspoon salt
1 Teaspoon mild, finely chopped onion
1/8 Teaspoon pepper
1 1/2 Tablespoon sugar
1/2 Cup salad oil

Peel and slice beets. Cover with cold water. Bring to a boil and cook until tender but still holding shape. Drain and set aside. Mix rest of ingredients in a jar with a lid. Shake vigorously until sugar has dissolved. Pour over hot beets. Cover and place in refrigerator until cold.

TWICE-BAKED STUFFED POTATOES

2 Large baking potatoes
1/2 Teaspoon salt
2 Tablespoon butter
1 Tablespoon chopped green onions

Bake potatoes. Slice lengthwise and scoop out inside, being careful not to damage skins. Mash with fork. Saute onions in butter until tender. Add other ingredients along with potatoes and stir. Spoon mixture back into skins and drizzle with a few drops of milk on each potato. Rough up with fork. Sprinkle with paprika. Return to oven and bake until nicely browned.

POTATO PANCAKES

1 1/2 Cups cold mashed potatoes
1 Egg, beaten
1 Tablespoon flour
Salt and pepper
1 Tablespoon grated green pepper
1/4 Cup chopped onion
Oil for frying

Mix potatoes, egg and flour. Add seasonings, green pepper and chopped onion. Shape into patties as you would hamburger. Place in hot oil and fry on medium heat. Brown both sides (about 5 minutes per side). Drain on paper towels.

SQUASH PUPPIES

2 Cups cooked squash, mashed
1 Large onion, chopped
1 Egg, beaten
1/4 Cup self-rising flour
1 Cup self-rising cornmeal
3 Tablespoons sugar
2 Teaspoons baking powder
1 Teaspoon salt
Dash cayenne pepper

Mix squash and finely chopped onion. Combine rest of ingredients. Drop by teaspoon into hot oil in deep fryer or heavy pan. Fry until nicely browned. Drain on paper towels. These will look like hush puppies. If batter is too stiff, add a little water.

SHUCKY BEANS

I guess Shucky Beans bring back some of the fondest memo-
ries from our childhood. Sissy would take fresh green beans
and with a large needle and stout white thread she would
"string the beans." As we got older, we were allowed to help.
It was the same procedure as stringing popcorn on thread for
a Christmas tree decoration except the two ends were tied
together to resemble a necklace. After the beans were strung,
she would hang them on the porch in the dry until they were
completely dried out. This took several weeks.

We have often talked about this, and how innovative people
had to be just to survive.

Things we took for granted as children, we now look back
on with wonder and the utmost respect.

1 String of Shucky beans
1 Handful of dried Pinto beans
1 Thick slice of fat back or streak o' lean
Enough water to cover

Break string and remove beans. Break them in half.
Rinse thoroughly several times (this is very important
due to them hanging out in the open). Place shucky
beans and Pinto beans in pot and cover with water. Soak
overnight. Drain, cover with water and bring to boil on
high. Reduce heat to medium, add fat back and cook
until both beans are tender. Excellent with cornbread,
green onions and cantaloupe.

STUFFED GREEN PEPPERS
(Meatless)

6 Large green peppers
Salt and pepper to taste
2 Heaping tablespoons grated cheese
1 Tablespoon chopped parsley
1 Tablespoon chopped onion
2 Small tomatoes, chopped
1 Cup cooked rice

Wash peppers tops, seeds and membrane. Parboil for 5 minutes. Mix other ingredients and stuff peppers with mixture. Place stuffed peppers into large muffin pan. Pour in cold water to half cover the peppers. Bake at 350 degrees for 30 minutes.

BAKED BEANS

Boil 2 cups of Northern beans until tender and then follow this recipe.

1. Layer of beans
2. Sprinkling of finely chopped onions
3. Sprinkling of dry mustard
4. Sprinkling of brown sugar
5. Pour a little tomatoes over each layer
6. Repeat layers until everything is used, finishing with tomatoes
7. Place several slices of bacon or salt pork on top

These are delicious cooked in an old crock bean pot. If you don't have one, use a deep casserole. Bake in a slow oven about 300 degrees for 1 1/2 to 2 hours or until juice is thick and bubbly and meat is thoroughly cooked.

CANDIED YAMS

2 16oz Can yams
2 Cups light brown sugar
1 1/2 Teaspoons cinnamon
1 Stick butter
1 Small can pineapple tidbits

Combine ingredients (do not drain yams or pineapple). In a medium saucepan, heat just until butter melts. Pour into casserole dish and bake at 400 degrees for 45 minutes to 1 hour. Sauce should be thick and bubbling.

FLUFFY WHIPPED POTATOES

4-5 Large potatoes
Water to cover
1 Teaspoon salt
1 Tablespoon margarine
1/4 Cup milk
1/4 Cup reserved liquid

Peel and dice potatoes. Place in saucepan and cover with cold water. Add salt. Cook until tender. Drain, reserving 1/4 cup of liquid. Whip potatoes with mixer. Add rest of ingredients in order listed. Whip between each addition. Serve hot.

TURNIP GREENS WITH POOR SOLDIERS

Greens:
Fresh turnip greens
Ham or streak o 'lean (to suit your needs)
Water to cover

Boil greens just until tender. Add ham or streak o' lean and continue to cook on medium low heat for about an hour. Add water if they start to boil dry.

Poor Soldiers:
1 Cup plain cornmeal
Red pepper to taste, optional
Teaspoon salt

Combine ingredients, stirring together well. Add enough pot liquor to make a stiff dough. Shape into small balls and flatten with fingers until 1/2-inch thick. Place on top of greens that are boiling. Reduce heat and simmer for 20 minutes.

In different parts of the country the dumplings have different names, such as cornbread dumplin's, corn dodgers, and of course, from our mountain home, poor soldiers. But whatever the name, they're delicious in any type of greens pot liquor or meat stock. This is one of our sister, Sandy's recipes.

FRIED GREEN TOMATOES

3-4 Green tomatoes
Cornmeal
Salt to taste
Shortening

While washing and slicing tomatoes, melt shortening in heavy frying pan. Add salt to cornmeal and mix well. Slice tomatoes in 1/4-inch slices. Roll in cornmeal. Drop carefully into melted, hot shortening. Reduce heat to medium high. Brown on both sides. Drain on paper towels.

ZUCCHINI PANCAKES

2 Cups shredded zucchini
1 1/2 Tablespoons chopped onion
2 Teaspoons chopped parsley
Salt and pepper to taste
1/4 Teaspoon dried oregano
2 Tablespoons flour
2 Eggs, beaten

Combine zucchini and onion; mix well. Sprinkle flour and spices over zucchini and onion. Pour in egg, stirring well. Drop by serving spoon making pancakes into hot oil. Cook over medium heat, browning on both sides. Drain on paper towels.

FRIED OKRA

1-1 1/2 Pounds okra
1 Cup corn meal
1/4 Cup flour
Salt and pepper to taste
1 1/2 Cups oil

Rinse okra and slice. Combine cornmeal and flour in a bag. Shake to mix. Drop okra into bag and shake well to coat. Remove and shake off excess cornmeal. Place in hot oil and fry until golden brown. Drain on paper towels.

SCALLOPED TOMATOES

2 Cups tomatoes
1 Cup bread crumbs
2 Tablespoons margarine
1 Cup grated cheese
4 Tablespoons sugar
1/2 Teaspoon salt
1/2 Cup diced onion

Place half of bread crumbs in bottom of buttered casserole dish; set aside. Combine tomatoes, margarine, sugar, salt and onion in a saucepan. Heat until butter is melted. Spoon half of tomato mixture over layer of crumbs. Repeat steps, ending with tomatoes. Sprinkle with cheese and additional bread crumbs. Bake in 350-degree oven for 25-30 minutes or until cheese is bubbly and crumbs are nicely browned.

CORN PUDDING

4 Cups fresh cream style corn
1 Teaspoon salt
1/4 Teaspoon pepper
2 Tablespoon sugar
3 Eggs, slightly beaten
2 Cups milk
3 Tablespoons melted butter

Combine ingredients in order listed. Mix well. Pour into sprayed casserole dish. Bake in 375-degree oven for 45-50 minutes.

YAM SOUFFLE

1 Large can yams
1 Stick margarine
1 Cup light brown sugar
2 Eggs beaten
1 Cup evaporated milk

Beat ingredients together. Pour into shallow casserole dish. Bake at 375 degrees for 15 minutes.

Topping:
1 Cup crushed corn flakes
1/2 Cup flaked coconut
1 Stick butter, melted
1 Cup chopped pecans

Mix dry ingredients into melted butter. It will be crumbly. Sprinkle over top of souffle and return to oven for additional 15 minutes.

CABBAGE CASSEROLE

1 Medium head of cabbage
1 Can cream of mushroom soup
1/2 Soup can of milk
1/2 Cup grated Cheddar
1 Cup buttered bread crumbs
Salt and pepper to taste

Chop cabbage and cook in boiling salted water until crisp-tender. Drain thoroughly. Combine soup and milk. Place cabbage into a casserole dish that has been sprayed with non-stick spray. Pour soup and milk over and layer with cheese. Sprinkle bread crumbs on top. Bake at 350 degrees for 30-35 minutes.

FRIED CABBAGE

1/4 Cup bacon grease
6 Cups shredded cabbage
Salt and pepper to taste
1/2 Cup chopped green onions including blades

Heat bacon grease and add cabbage, salt, pepper and onions. Stir often while frying to avoid scorching. Fry until light brown.

PEPPER RELISH

1 Dozen red peppers
1 Dozen green peppers
12 Medium onions
1 Quart vinegar
2 Cups sugar
3 Tablespoons salt
1 Tablespoon mustard seed

Cut pepper in half and remove seeds and membrane. Coarsely chop peppers and onions by hand or in a food processor. Place in saucepan and cover with boiling water; drain. Cover with cold water and bring to boiling point; drain. Add vinegar, sugar salt and mustard seed; bring to a boil. Reduce heat and cook for 10 minutes. Spoon into jars and seal.

CORN RELISH

1 Dozen ears corn
1 Large onion
1 Small head cabbage
1 Green pepper
1 Red pepper
1 Large cucumber
1 1/2 Cup vinegar
1 1/2 Cup sugar
1 Tablespoon salt
1/4 Teaspoon turmeric

Boil enough water to cover corn. Bring to boil and drop corn in and allow to boil for one minute. Remove from water and set aside to cool. Chop onion, cabbage, peppers and cucumbers. Cut corn from cobs and add to vegetables Place vinegar, sugar, salt and turmeric in a heavy pot and bring to a boil. Add vegetables and continue to cook for 5 minutes, stirring constantly. Spoon into jars and seal.

OKRA AND RICE

4 Slices bacon
2 Cups fresh okra
1 Small onion, chopped
2 Cups cooked rice

Fry bacon until crisp. Remove from pan and drain on paper towels. Fry okra and onion in hot bacon grease until tender and light brown. Add cooked rice. Crumble bacon and add to rest of mixture. Stir well. Reduce heat and simmer until hot.

OKRA AND GREEN TOMATO FRITTERS

1/4 Cup flour
1/4 Cup cornmeal
1 Cup sliced okra, finely sliced
1/2 Cup chopped onion
1/2 Cup chopped green tomatoes
2 Eggs, beaten
Salt and pepper to taste
Oil for frying

Combine ingredients, mixing well. Drop by tablespoonful into hot oil. Fry until golden brown. Drain on paper towels.

STUFFED POTATOES

4 Large baking potatoes
1 Teaspoons chopped parsley
Salt and peer to taste
2 Tablespoons margarine
Paprika for garnish
1 Teaspoon milk for each potato

Wash and cover potatoes with cold water. Boil until done. Remove from water and let stand until cool enough to handle. Split each potato in half and remove insides from jacket, being careful not to tear. Mash potatoes and add salt, pepper, parsley and margarine. Toss with a fork until mixed and margarine is melted. Sprinkle milk over each potato. Spoon back into jackets and garnish with paprika. Bake in 450-degree oven until nicely browned. If desired, you can also garnish with crumbled bacon.

BAKED TOMATOES

3 Tomatoes, cut in half
2 Cups soft bread crumbs
2 Tablespoons butter or margarine
Salt and pepper to taste

Remove pulp from center of tomatoes and set aside. Fill halves with bread crumbs. Place on top of each half a teaspoon of hard butter or margarine. Bake in 450-degree oven for 20-30 minutes. Place pulp in blender and puree. To this, add 1-2 Tablespoons of sugar, (depending on sweetness desired) and 1 teaspoon butter.
Heat to boiling. Pour over tomato halves when ready

FRESH CREAM STYLE CORN

12 Ears of corn
2 Tablespoons sugar
4 Tablespoons of butter or melted fat
Salt to taste

Cut tops off kernels in a downward motion with a sharp knife. Scrape cob with flat side of blade (this removes rest of corn and milk). Combine ingredients in a heavy sauce pan. Cook on low heat until done. Stir frequently or it will stick. Delicious served with hot home-made biscuits.

CREAMED PEAS AND CARROTS

1 16 oz. Can green peas
1 16 oz. Can sliced carrots
2 Tablespoons margarine
Cup cold milk
2 Tablespoons flour
Salt and pepper to taste

Bring peas, carrots and margarine to boil. Cook until heated through. Pour milk into a cup and beat in flour, salt and pepper with a fork until lumps are dissolved. Pour slowly into boiling peas and carrots a little at a time until desired thickness. For variety, pour in a can of drained tuna and serve over toast.

HOPPIN' JOHN

1 16 oz. Can blackeyed peas
1 Cup ham, chopped
1 Cup onion, chopped fine
2 Tablespoons oil
1/2 Teaspoon salt
3 Cups cooked rice

Saute ham and onion in the oil. Combine peas and rice. Add to ham and onion and simmer for 5-10 minutes.

PINTO BEANS

1 Pound pinto beans
Enough water to cover
1-Inch thick slice of fat back

Go through beans and pick out debris. Rinse with cold water three times. In a heavy saucepan, cover with water and bring to boil on high. Reduce to medium, add meat and cover. Cook until tender and juice is thick. Add water as needed.

BABY LIMAS

1 Pound baby lima beans
Enough water to cover
Ham bone or plenty of ham

Check beans for any foreign matter. Rinse three times in cold water. Cover with cold water and add bone or ham. Bring to boil on high heat. Reduce to medium heat; cook until tender. Add water as needed.

MAIN COURSES & CASSEROLES

"Never cook in a hurry, or you'll have frustration and worry."

~ SOUTHERN LADIES ~ KNOW HOW TO COOK IT!

COOKING HINTS

A Mother's Prayer

I pray for your peace of mind.
Stay in God's favor and this you'll find.
I pray for your safety on life's highway.
Buckle up and ride with the Master
every day.
I pray for your happiness and a heart
that's light.
Your problems He'll take care of,
talk to Him every night.
I pray for your assurance that comes from within.
The confidence He'll give you,
He's your very best friend.

CHICKEN AND DUMPLIN'S

1 4-5 Pound hen
Water to cover
Salt and pepper taste

Dumplin's:
3 Cups self rising flour
2 Egg yolks (optional)
Water

Cut up hen and rinse. Place in a large pot with enough water to cover. Add salt and pepper. Cover and cook until meat is tender and pulls away from bones. Remove from broth and allow to cool while making dumplin's. In a bowl, combine the flour, yolks and enough water to make a very thick paste. Drop paste by serving spoon onto a heavily floured pastry cloth or board. Fold over repeatedly until a stiff ball forms. Roll out with floured rolling pin until thickness desired. Cut into strips and then squares. Repeat until all dough has been used. Bring stock to a boil again and drop in dumplin's one at a time until all are used. Reduce heat and cook for 10 minutes. De-bone chicken and add to dumplin's; cook additional 5 minutes on medium heat. Don't overcook.

Hint: While cutting dumplin's, place a piece of wax paper between each layer to keep them from sticking together

STEW BEEF AND BROWN GRAVY

2 Pounds stew beef, not lean
Water to cover
1/4 Cup flour
Salt and pepper to taste
3 Cups water for gravy

Rinse beef and place in a large pot. Sprinkle with salt and pepper. Cover with water. Cover and cook over medium heat until tender. Remove cover and cook until dry and only grease from meat is in bottom of pot. Remove meat and stir in flour. Add more fat if needed. Stir until brown (add more salt and pepper, if desired). Add meat to flour and grease and continue to fry until flour is deep brown. Pour water over meat. Stir well until gravy thickness. Cover and reduce heat. Simmer for 15-20 minutes. Good with white rice or mashed potatoes.

DOUBLE BOILER MEAT LOAF

1 1/2 Pounds ground beef
1/2 Cup chopped onion
1/4 Cup chopped bell pepper
1/2 Teaspoon salt
1/8 Teaspoon pepper
1 Cup fine rolled crackers
1 Egg, beaten
1 Cup milk
1 Tablespoon
   Worcestershire sauce
2 1/2 Cups tomato sauce

Combine ingredients except tomato sauce; mix well. Into top of a double boiler, pour 1 cup of tomato sauce. Press in half of meat mixture. Add another cup of sauce and press in other half of meat mixture. Pour remainder of sauce over. Cover and steam over boiling water for 3 hours or until completely done. Remove meat and pour the sauce from the double boiler over. CAUTION: Contains ground meat, cook until completely done.

CHICKEN AND DRESSING WITH GRAVY

1 2-3 pound chicken
1 Large cake cornbread
3 Chopped onions
Salt and pepper to taste
4 Eggs
Sage to taste
Chicken stock

Boil chicken until tender in a large pot. Be sure to add a lot of water so you'll have enough broth. Remove chicken and allow to cool. Remove meat from bones and proceed with recipe. Crumble insides of cornbread (no crust). Add chicken along with rest of ingredients and mix thoroughly. Add enough stock to make it good and wet. Spoon into an oblong baking pan and bake at 375 degrees until nicely browned.

Gravy:
4 Cups broth
2 Teaspoons cornstarch
2 Tablespoons water
2 Hard boiled eggs
Cooked giblets
Salt and pepper to taste

Bring broth to a boil. Stir cornstarch, salt and pepper into 2 tablespoons of water. Add to broth. Cook until thickened. Chop eggs and giblets. Add to gravy and simmer 5 minutes.

HAM AND CHEESE CASSEROLE

1 Small package elbow macaroni
1 1/2 Cups cooked ground ham
1 3/4 Cups Cheddar cheese, divided
1 Can evaporated milk
2 Tablespoons margarine
1 Egg, beaten

Cook macaroni in boiling salted water until tender. Drain and stir in margarine. Combine ham and half of cheese. Mix well. Stir into macaroni. Pour into a casserole dish. Beat egg and milk together. Pour over top of mixture and cover with remaining cheese. Bake in a 400-degree oven for 30-35 minutes. Cheese should be golden brown.

HAMBURGER CASSEROLE

1 Pound hamburger
1 Onion, chopped
3 Cups cooked potatoes
2 Cups grated cheese
1 Can cream of mushroom soup
1/2 Soup can water

Fry hamburger and onion until done; drain. Place hamburger on bottom of casserole, cover with potatoes and then cheese. Mix soup and water. Pour over top. Bake in a 350-degree oven for 35-40 minutes.

RICE AND BOLOGNA CASSEROLE

1/2 Cup dry rice
1 Cup cubed bologna
2 Cups tomatoes
4 Tablespoons butter
1 Tablespoon chopped onion
1 Tablespoon chopped bell pepper
1 Teaspoon salt
1/2 Teaspoon pepper

Melt butter in a frying pan and add rice, bologna and onion. Allow to cook over a low heat until meat, onion and rice are equally light brown. Add seasonings, green pepper and tomatoes. Cover and simmer for 50-60 minutes.

TUNA NOODLE CASSEROLE

1 6-oz Can tuna, drained
1 Small package egg noodles, cooked and drained
1 Can mushroom soup
1 Can of milk (soup can)
1/4 Stick margarine
1 Cup bread crumbs

Combine first five ingredients, mixing well. Pour into casserole dish that has been sprayed with non-stick spray. Sprinkle bread crumbs on top and dot with margarine. Bake in 375-degree oven 35-40 minutes or until nicely browned.

LIVER AND ONION GRAVY

1 Pound sliced liver
1 Cup self-rising flour
1/2 Teaspoon salt
1/2 Teaspoon black pepper
Oil for frying

Gravy:
3 Tablespoons flour
1/2 Teaspoon salt
1/2 Teaspoon pepper
1 Large onion, chopped

Rinse liver and beat with mallet until thin. Combine flour, salt and pepper. Roll liver in flour mixture and fry until brown on both sides and tender. Drain on paper towels. Leave about 1/3 cup of drippings in pan and stir in flour, salt and pepper until smooth. Add onions; cook until tender. Stir in enough water for desired thickness. Continue to cook for 2 more minutes. Return liver to gravy and simmer for about 30 minutes. Excellent over rice or mashed potatoes.

LIVER LOAF

1 Pound liver
3 Slices bacon, crumbled
3 Tablespoons chopped onion
1 Green pepper, chopped
1 Medium tomato, chopped
1/2 Cup milk
1 Egg, beaten
1 Cup bread crumbs
1 Teaspoon salt
1/4 Teaspoon pepper
Pinch of parsley

Drop liver into boiling water and cook until done. Remove and grind in food processor. Combine bacon, pepper, onion, tomato and bread. Add egg and seasonings to bread mixture and mix well. Mix in milk and liver. Pour into greased bread pan and bake at 350 degrees for 40-45 minutes.

MEATLOAF

2 Pounds ground chuck
1 Large onion, chopped
1 Bell pepper, chopped
15 Saltine crackers
2 Eggs, beaten
1 Can tomato soup

Mix ingredients thoroughly with hands. Place in square baking dish. Bake at 400 degrees for 1 1/2 hours or until completely done (make sure completely cooked, due to being made from ground beef). While baking, pour off excess grease. The last 15 minutes of baking, cover with tomato ketchup.

BAR-B-QUED SPARE RIBS

5 Pounds spare ribs
Garlic salt and ginger to taste
1 Cup ketchup
1/4 Cup vinegar
1 Tablespoon soy sauce
1/4 Cup brown sugar
1/4 Cup Worcestershire sauce
1 Small onion, chopped
1 Green pepper, chopped
1 Small can crushed pineapple

Use enough garlic salt and ginger to sprinkle over ribs. In a frying pan heat enough oil to brown ribs. After browning, drain off oil. Combine rest of ingredients to make sauce. Pour over ribs that have been removed from heat. Let stand 10-15 minutes. Return to heat and cook until tender.

SMOTHERED CHICKEN

10-12 pieces chicken
Enough flour for rolling
Shortening for frying
Salt and pepper to taste
1 Can cream of mushroom soup
1 Soup can of milk

Combine flour, salt and pepper. Rinse chicken thoroughly and pat dry. Roll in flour mixture and brown on all sides in hot shortening. Remove chicken to a roasting pan. Pour soup and milk into drippings and bring to a boil. Pour over chicken and cover. Bake in a 325 degree oven for 1 1/2 hours or until done. Uncover for the last 30 minutes.

CHICKEN CASSEROLE

4 Cups cooked diced chicken
2 Small carrots, sliced
1/2 Can peas
1/2 Can whole kernel corn
1 Small onion,chopped fine
1 Can mushroom soup
1/2 Cup salad dressing
1/2 Cup milk
Salt and pepper to taste
1 Cup grated cheese
1/2 Cup crushed potato chips

Combine first 9 ingredients, mixing well. Pour into sprayed casserole dish. Cover with cheese and sprinkle on potato chips. Bake at 350 degrees for 50 minutes to 1 hour.

QUICK PORK CHOP CASSEROLE

4-6 Pork chops
1 Cup rice
1 Envelope onion soup mix
Oil for browning
1 Can cream of chicken soup
1 1/2 Soup can water

Brown chops on both sides in oil. Place rice in bottom of sprayed casserole dish. Sprinkle on onion soup mix. Place pork chops on top. Pour soup and water over chops. Bake in a 375-degree oven for 1 hour.

HAM AND YAMS

1 Center-cut ham slice
1 1/2 Cups mashed yams
1/2 Cup apple sauce
1/2 Teaspoon cinnamon
3 Tablespoons lemon juice
1/2 Cup packed brown sugar
1/2 Stick butter

Place ham in bottom of baking dish. Combine rest of ingredients, except butter, mixing well. Spoon over ham slice and dot with butter. Bake in a 325 degree oven for 1 hour.

BAKED CHICKEN LIVERS

16 Chicken livers
Salt and pepper
8 Slices bacon cut in half

Rinse and drain livers. Salt and pepper. Wrap 1/2 slice of bacon around each liver, overlapping the ends. Hold together with toothpick. Place on oblong baking pan in single layer. Bake at 400 degrees for 30-35 minutes. Bacon should be completely browned. We use these for meals and appetizers.

SKILLET CHOPS & GRAVY

4-6 Lean pork chops
Salt and pepper
1/4 Cup oil
1 Can mushroom soup
1/2 Can evaporated milk
1/4 Cup water

Rinse and dry chops. Salt and pepper. Fry in hot oil, browning on both sides. Cover and continue to cook until done. Remove and drain on paper towels. Pour off drippings, leaving one tablespoon. Stir in soup, milk and water; stir well. Return chops to gravy. Cover and simmer for 15 minutes.

BATTER-FRIED PORK CHOPS

4-6 Center cut chops
Flour for rolling
Salt and pepper to taste
2/3 Cup oil

Rinse and pat dry chops. Add salt and pepper to flour, mixing well. Roll chops in flour. Heat oil. Carefully place chops in hot oil. Cover and fry, browning on both sides. Cook until completely done, about 10-15 minutes per side depending on thickness of chop. Delicious served with stewed tomatoes and white rice.

HAMBURGER STEAKS AND GRAVY

1 1/2 Pounds hamburger
1 Large onion, chopped and divided
3 Tablespoons flour
Salt and pepper to taste

Add half the chopped onion, salt and pepper into hamburger and mix well. Make into 4 to 6-oz. patties. Fry in a heavy frying pan until done (due to being ground meat, cook completely). Remove from pan and drain on paper towels. Pour off grease, leaving about a 1/4 cup in pan. To this, stir in flour, salt, pepper and rest of onion. Stir constantly until a deep brown and onion is tender. Stir in 2 1/2 to 3 cups water until desired thickness is reached. Return hamburger to gravy. Cover and simmer 15-20 minutes.

COUNTRY STYLE STEAK

1 1/2 Pounds cube steak
Flour for rolling
Salt and pepper to taste

2/3 Cup oil
1 Medium onion, chopped

Rinse and pat steak dry with paper towels. Pound with mallet. Roll in flour that salt and pepper has been added too. Heat oil and add steak carefully. Brown on both sides and cook until done. Remove from oil onto paper towels to drain. Add 3 tablespoons flour and onion into drippings and stir constantly until deep brown and onion is tender. Stir in 2 1/2 cups water and continue stirring until thickened. Return steak to gravy and simmer 20-25 minutes.

STEW AND DUMPLIN'S

2 Pounds lean beef
4 Cups potatoes
1 1/2 Cup carrots
1 Cup canned tomatoes
2 Onions, chopped

2 Teaspoons salt
1/4 Teaspoon pepper
1 Tablespoon flour
2 Tablespoons chopped parsley

Rinse meat and place in large pot along with salt and pepper. Cover with hot water and cook on medium heat until tender, about 1 1/2 hours. Add vegetables the last 1/2 hour of cooking.

Dumplin's:
2 Teaspoons baking powder
1 Cup flour
1/2 Teaspoon salt

1 Teaspoon shortening
Cold water

Sift together flour, baking powder and salt. Knead in shortening, along with enough water to make dough hold together. Drop by spoonfuls into boiling stew.

SAUSAGE AND CABBAGE

1 Pound smoked sausage
1 Head cabbage
1/2 Cup chopped onion
Salt and pepper to taste

Start by slicing sausage into 1/2-inch slices. In a pot add water to cover; cook while preparing vegetables. Shred cabbage and chop onions. Add vegetables to pot and continue to cook until tender.

SAUSAGE AND RICE CASSEROLE

1 Pound sausage
1 Large onion, chopped
1 Can cream of mushroom soup
1/2 Soup can water
1/2 Cup uncooked rice
Salt and pepper to taste

In a large skillet, brown sausage and onion until done; drain. Add soup, water, rice, salt and pepper. Cook for several minutes. Pour into greased casserole dish and bake at 400 degrees for 25-30 minutes.

HAMBURGER STEAK WITH CHEESE

2 Pounds hamburger
1 Can mushroom soup, undiluted
4 Slices cheese
Salt and pepper

Make four large patties from hamburger. Place in sprayed baking dish. Pour soup over patties, along with salt and pepper. Cook at 350 degrees 35-40 minutes (be sure completely cooked due to being ground meat). Remove from oven and place a slice of cheese on top of each patty. Return to oven and bake additional 5 minutes. Remove patties to platter. Stir soup and serve on side. You can change dish by adding garlic, green pepper or onions. Use your imagination.

CHICKEN FRIED STEAK

1 Pound round steak
1 Egg
2 Teaspoons milk
1 Cup flour
Salt and pepper to taste
Oil for cooking

Beat steak with mallet until about 1/4-inch thick. Combine flour, salt and pepper. Cut steak into serving-size pieces. Beat egg and milk together. Dip steak in egg and milk mixture. Roll in flour. Brown in hot oil on both sides. Cover and reduce heat. Cook on low heat for 1 hour or until tender.

BAKED CHICKEN SALAD

2 1/2 Cups cooked, chopped chicken
1 Can cream of chicken soup
1 Cup mayonnaise
1/2 Cup chopped celery
1/2 Cup chopped green pepper
1 Tablespoon grated, mild onion
1 1/2 Tablespoons lemon juice
2 Tablespoons Worcestershire sauce
1 Cup grated Cheddar cheese

Combine ingredients; mix well. Pour into greased casserole dish. Bake at 400 degrees for 40-45 minutes or until nicely browned.

SMOKED SAUSAGE AND CHILI CORN

1-1 1/2 Pound smoked sausage
1/4 Cup finely chopped onion
1/4 Cup finely chopped green pepper
2 Tablespoons oil
1 1/2 Cups canned tomatoes
1 Cup kidney beans
Salt to taste
Dash of pepper
1/4 Teaspoon chili powder
1 Can whole kernel corn

Fry sausage and place on paper towels to drain. Fry onion and green pepper in oil. Add tomatoes, beans and seasonings. Reduce heat and simmer for 15 minutes. Drain corn and add to mixture. Simmer 15 minutes more, stirring frequently. Turn into a serving dish. Arrange smoked sausage on top.

BAR-B-QUE CHICKEN

4 Tablespoons orange juice
4 Tablespoons Worcestershire sauce
1/2 Cup water
Salt and pepper to taste
4 Tablespoon vinegar
4 Tablespoons ketchup
4 Tablespoons brown sugar
3 Tablespoons bacon drippings
2 1/2 Pounds chicken parts

Rinse and pat chicken dry. Place in bottom of baking pan. Combine ingredients for sauce in a sauce pan. Simmer 10 minutes in order for flavors to mingle. Pour light coating over chicken and bake uncovered in a 350-degree oven for 1 1/2 hours. Baste with additional sauce while baking.

HOMINY AND CHICKEN CASSEROLE

1 Large can hominy
1 Can cream of chicken soup
1/2 Cup chopped onion
2 Cups grated cheese
1 Can cream of mushroom soup
1/2 Cup chopped celery
1/2 Cup chopped bell pepper
1 Teaspoon salt
1 Cup cubed cooked chicken
2 Eggs, beaten

Saute onion, celery and pepper in 2 Tablespoons butter until just tender; drain. Add remaining ingredients and mix well. Pour into casserole dish and bake at 350 degrees for 30-35 minutes.

CHICKEN LIVERS AND GRAVY

1 Container chicken livers
1 1/2 Cups flour for shaking
Salt and pepper to taste
Oil for frying

Clean and rinse livers; drain well. Pour flour, salt and pepper into a bag; shake well. Drop livers into bag a few at a time and shake to coat. Drop into hot oil and pierce with fork to lessen grease spattering. Brown on both sides and fry until completely done. Remove livers from oil onto paper towels to drain. Add enough flour (salt and pepper if desired) to oil to make a loose paste, stirring constantly until deep brown. Add water and stir until thickened to desired consistency. Return livers to gravy; cover and simmer 10-15 minutes.

ORIENTAL CHICKEN LIVERS

1 Pound chicken livers
1/4 Cup soy sauce
2 Tablespoons brown sugar
1/2 Teaspoon chopped garlic
1/4 Teaspoon ginger
1/4 Cup oil

Clean and rinse livers ; drain and set aside. In a bowl, combine soy sauce, brown sugar, chopped garlic and ginger, stirring well. Add livers and stir lightly to coat. Cover and refrigerate for several hours. When ready to fry, drain off sauce and dry livers with paper towels. Place carefully in hot oil, piercing liver with fork to reduce grease spattering. Brown on both sides until completely done.

BAKED HAM WITH RAISIN SAUCE

10- to 12-Pound ham
1 Cup brown sugar
24 Cloves
1/4 Cup vinegar
Teaspoon dry mustard

Place ham fat side up on baking rack in pan. Bake uncovered in a 325-degree oven for 18-20 minutes per pound. Last half hour of baking, remove the rind, score fat into diamond shapes and stud with cloves. Mix brown sugar, vinegar, and dry mustard. Cover ham with this. Continue to bake until sugar browns and glazes.

Sauce:
1/2 Cup raisins
1/4 Teaspoon salt
1/8 Teaspoon cloves
1 Tablespoon ham fat
Juice of one orange
Juice of one lemon
1/4 Teaspoon cinnamon
1/2 Cup brown sugar
2 Teaspoons corn starch

Soak raisins in 1 1/2 cups water for 1/2 hour. Cook in same water for 15 minutes. Add orange and lemon juice along with rind of orange. Mix spices with sugar and corn starch. To this, add small amount of cold water. Pour into raisins while water is boiling. Stir until thickened. Add fat and serve hot.

BAKED FRIED CHICKEN

2-3 Pounds fryer pieces
1 Cup milk
1 Cup crushed corn flakes
Salt and pepper to taste

Rinse chicken and pat dry with paper towels. Wet chicken in milk. Roll in corn flakes crumbs. Place on greased baking pan. Bake at 400 degrees until golden brown and completely done, turning once halfway through baking.

CHICKEN CROQUETTES

1/2 Cup margarine
1/4 Cup flour
2 Teaspoons scraped onions
Salt and pepper to taste
1/2 Teaspoon poultry seasoning
1 Cup milk
1 1/2 Tablespoons parsley flakes
2 Cups diced cooked chicken
1 Egg and 1 Cup bread crumbs

Melt margarine. Add flour, stirring well until lumps have dissolved. Add onions and seasonings, stirring constantly. Pour in milk and cook until thickened. Add chicken and parsley. Allow to cool completely. Shape into oblong (2 1/2-inch) croquettes. Slightly beat egg and add 2 tablespoons of milk. Dip each croquet into this and roll in the bread crumbs. Fry in deep hot fat until golden brown.

CHICKEN BOG

2-3 Pounds chicken parts
1 Pound smoked sausage
1/2 Pound chicken gizzards
1 Small onion, chopped
8 Cups water
4 Cups rice
Salt and pepper to taste

Clean and rinse gizzards. Rinse chicken and place in heavy large pot along with gizzards and sliced sausage (slice sausage about 1/2 inch thick). Add water, onion, salt and pepper. Cover with water and cook until tender. Remove chicken pieces from broth and allow to cool. De-bone chicken and return to broth. Add more water to bring back up to 8 cups of broth. Bring to a quick boil and add rice. Reduce heat to low. Cook for 20 minutes or until broth is absorbed and rice is tender.

FRIED FAT BACK

1 Pound slab fat back
Water to cover

Rinse fat back and slice, place in a large, heavy frying pan. Cover with water; boil. Allow to boil for 2-3 minutes. Drain off water. Return to heat. Fry on both sides until grease is cooked out and fat back is crispy. Drain on paper towels.

MACARONI AND CHEESE PIE

1 8oz. Package elbow macaroni
1 1/2 Cup sharp Cheddar cheese, grated
2 Eggs, beaten
2 Cups evaporated milk
Salt and pepper to taste
3 Tablespoons butter or margarine

Cook macaroni according to package directions. Drain. Place half of macaroni on bottom of a 2-quart casserole dish. Layer with 3/4 cup cheese. Repeat, ending with cheese. Mix together milk and eggs, pour over and dot with butter or margarine. Bake in 350-degree oven 35-40 minutes or until bubbly and cheese is nicely browned.

POTATO CASSEROLE

1 8oz. Carton sour cream
1 Cup cream of chicken soup
1/4 Cup melted margarine
1 Cup grated Cheddar cheese
1/2 Cup chopped onion
2 Cups crushed corn flakes
4-5 medium potatoes

Peel and slice enough Irish potatoes to fill an 8x8 baking dish a little more than half full. Boil until done and drain. Pour into casserole and set aside. Combine above ingredients, except corn flakes, mixing well. Pour over potatoes and top with corn flakes. Bake in 350-degree oven 45-50 minutes.

FRIED RABBIT OR SQUIRREL

1 Rabbit or squirrel
Flour for rolling
Salt and pepper to taste
Oil for frying

Wash dressed meat thoroughly. Cut legs at joint. Split down center back through the breast, and cut into two pieces. Place in heavy pot and cover with water, along with salt and pepper. Bring to boil. Reduce heat to medium and cook for about 1 1/2 hours or until tender. Remove from heat. Lift meat out of pot and drain on paper towels.

In a cast iron frying pan, heat oil. While oil is heating, roll meat in flour that salt and pepper has been added to. Carefully place meat in hot oil and brown on all sides. Drain on paper towels.

TRUE SOUTHERN FRIED CHICKEN

1 Fryer, cut up
2 Cups self-rising flour
Salt and pepper to taste
Shortening for frying

While preparing chicken, melt shortening in a deep, heavy frying pan (cast iron is excellent). You'll need enough to cover chicken halfway. Rinse chicken and leave damp. Combine flour, salt and pepper in a bag. Shake to mix. Drop chicken in a few pieces at a time. Shake to coat. When shortening is hot, carefully place chicken in pan. Cover and cook on medium. Brown on both sides (10-15 minutes per side). Remove and drain on paper towels. Good hot or cold.

CHILI WITH BEANS

1 Pound ground beef
1 Can kidney beans
1 Large chopped onion
1 Chopped green pepper
3 Cups tomatoes
1 1/4 Teaspoons salt
1/8 Teaspoon cayenne pepper
3 Garlic cloves, chopped fine
1 Bay leaf
1-2 Tablespoons chili powder

Brown ground beef, onion and pepper. Drain off excess grease. To tomatoes, add seasonings. Combine all ingredients except beans and simmer for 1 1/2-2 hours. You may need to add a little water if mixture starts drying out. Drain beans, pour into meat sauce and heat through. Remove bay leaf. Pour into individual bowls and top with grated sharp Cheddar cheese.

COUNTRY HAM AND RED EYE GRAVY

1/4-1/2" slices of country ham
1/2 to 1 cup strong black coffee

Rinse ham and pat dry. Slice fat so ham won't curl while frying. Place in lightly oiled frying pan and cook slowly. Brown on both sides. Drain on paper towels and transfer to a warm platter (if it gets cold, it will be tough). Pour coffee into drippings and cook until it turns red. Amount of coffee depends on drippings. For a small amount of drippings, use 1/2 cup and for large amount, use 1 cup. Great for sopping with homemade buttermilk biscuits or over grits.

FRIED TURKEY

2 Gallons peanut oil
10-12 Pound turkey
Louisiana Cajun Spice to taste

For this you will need a 16-quart pot with a basket and a propane cooker to cook on outside.

The day before, rinse thawed turkey. Do not dry. On enough aluminum foil to wrap turkey in, place bird in center. Sprinkle with as much seasoning as you like and rub in well. Wrap bird tightly and place in refrigerator until ready to use.

Heat oil until hot, about 350 degrees. Carefully lower turkey into hot oil. Keep heat up while cooking. Cook until done (usually 45-50 minutes). It should be golden brown.

POT ROAST

3-4 Pound chuck roast
Flour for rolling + 3 heaping tbls,
Salt and pepper to taste
1/2 Cup oil
2 Onions, sliced
5 Potatoes, peeled and cut in half
3 Carrots cut into 1" pieces

Rinse roast and pat dry with paper towels. Add salt and pepper to flour, mixing well. Sprinkle flour mixture over roast covering entirely. Heat oil in large heavy pot. Place roast in hot oil and brown on both sides. Remove from oil. Add 3 tablespoons flour to oil along with salt and pepper if desired. Stir constantly until flour is deep brown. Pour in 2 cups of water, stirring constantly until thickened. Return roast to gravy and cover. Cook on medium heat about 1 1/2 hours. Add prepared vegetables the last 1/2 hour of cooking and cook until meat and vegetables are tender. Add water if needed.

Helpful hint: When you have leftovers containing gravy, add a small amount of water when reheating to thin.

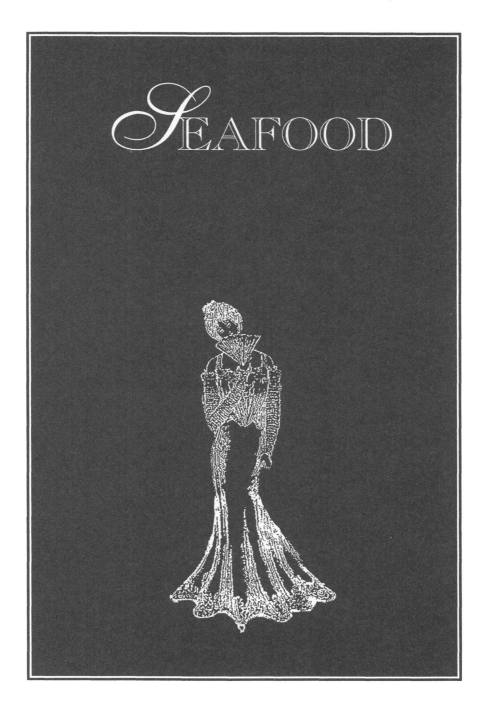

SEAFOOD

"Things we took for
granted as children,
we now
look back on with wonder
and the utmost respect."

FOOD FOR THOUGHT

Your yesterdays are memories now,
and today's will be tomorrow's
all of your happy times, and yes,
even your sorrows.

So each day as you start afresh be
sure you keep in mind,
how good the Lord has been to you
so be thoughtful loving and kind.

HOPE

As you walk along life's highway
and everything seems up hill,
just ask The Lord to lift you up
and He promises, He will!

When things get so difficult and
you've reached the end of your
rope.
Don't let go! Just hang on! As long
as there's breath there's hope!

Copyright 1997
Sharen A. Strickland

CHARLIE'S STUFFED SHRIMP

12 Jumbo shrimp
12 Slices bacon
1/4 Cup minced yellow onion
1/4 Cup minced green bell pepper
1/8 Cup minced red bell pepper or pimentos
1- 8 oz. Can lump crab meat
1/4 Cup mayonnaise + 1/8 cup Grey Poupon
1 Teaspoon Old Bay seasoning
1/2 Teaspoon cayenne pepper
1/2 Cup bread crumbs
1/2 Teaspoon tarragon
1/2 Cup water
Salt and pepper to taste
1/2 Cup Cheddar and Mozzarella cheese, optional

Peel, de-vein and butterfly shrimp; place in a bowl and
cover with milk until ready to stuff. In a large mixing
bowl, combine onion, green and red pepper or pimento,
crab meat, mayonnaise, mustard, Old Bay seasoning,
cayenne pepper, bread crumbs, water, salt and pepper;
mix well. Take a shrimp in one hand and with a teaspoon, spoon mixture into the shrimp. Wrap with a slice
of bacon; secure with toothpick. Continue procedure
until all shrimp are stuffed. Bake uncovered at 400
degrees (pre-heated) for 35-40 minutes. If cheese is used,
after specified cooking time, remove from oven, sprinkle
with cheese, and return to oven until melted.

As per Charlie: Serve with your favorite steamed vegetables, crescent rolls and a nice Chardonnay. Enjoy!

*Charlie is a nephew (Sharon's). He is a certified chef and this
is one of his truly great recipes. We say; this is definitely a keep-
er!!! One of our favorites!*

SALMON ROLL

ROLL:
2 Cups flour
4 Teaspoons baking powder
1/2 Teaspoon salt
4 Tablespoons shortening
1 Egg
1/2 Cup milk

FILLING:
1 Can salmon
4 Tablespoons milk
2 Tablespoons lemon juice
2 Teaspoons scraped onion
1 1/2 Tablespoons chopped parsley
1/2 Teaspoon salt

Sift together first 3 ingredients. Add shortening, mixing well. Beat egg in a measuring cup, adding milk to make 3/4 cup. Add to first mixture to form a dough. Turn out onto floured pastry board. Roll into an 8- or 9-inch triangle, leaving about 1/4" thick. Mix together ingredients for filling (be sure to remove skin and bones from salmon and flake). Spread evenly on dough. Roll up as you would a jelly roll. Place on baking sheet and bake for 30 minutes at 425 degrees. Cool slightly before slicing. Serve with clam sauce.

Clam sauce:
1 Small can condensed clam chowder (soup section at grocers)
1/3 Cup milk

Combine soup and milk. Bring to boil, stirring constantly.

SEAFOOD CASSEROLE

1/2 Pound crab meat, flaked
1/2 Pound shrimp, cleaned
1/2 Teaspoon salt
1 Teaspoon Worcestershire sauce
2 Eggs, beaten
1 Medium green pepper, chopped
1 Medium onion, chopped
1 Cup chopped celery
1 Cup mayonnaise
1 Can clam chowder

Combine ingredients, mixing well. Pour into greased casserole dish. Bake at 350 degrees 35-40 minutes. Top should be a nice brown.

SALMON TIMBALES

1 Can salmon
1 Cup soft bread crumbs
1/4 Cup milk
2 Eggs, beaten
1 Tablespoon chopped onion
Salt and pepper to taste

Drain salmon and remove skin and bones. Flake and mix with rest of ingredients. Place in greased custard cups. Bake in a 350-degree oven for 30 minutes. Serve with your favorite cheese sauce.

SCALLOPED SALMON

1 Pound can salmon
1 1/2 Cups milk
2 Tablespoons butter
3/4 Teaspoon salt
2 Tablespoons flour
1 Cup bread crumbs

Drain salmon. Remove dark skin and bones. Prepare a sauce of fat, flour, milk and salt. Place a layer of salmon on bottom of greased baking dish. Add some sauce, then another layer of salmon, and so on until all ingredients are used. Cover top with bread crumbs dotted with butter. Bake at 350 degrees until sauce bubbles and crumbs are brown.

LOBSTER WIGGLE

1 Pound lobster
1 Can peas
3 Cups milk
1 Tablespoon flour
Butter, size of an egg
Red pepper and salt

Pour milk in a heavy saucepan. Shred lobster, drain peas and add both to milk. Stir flour in 3 Tablespoons cold water until lumps are dissolved. Pour into mixture along with butter. Add red pepper and salt to suit taste. Cook until thickened.

SALMON STEW

1 16oz. Can salmon
2 Cups whole milk
2 Cups evaporated milk
4 Tablespoons butter or margarine
Salt and pepper to taste

Drain salmon and remove bones and dark skin.
Crumble with a fork. Place in a medium-sized sauce pan
and add salmon, butter, salt and pepper. Bring to a slow
boil over medium heat. Reduce heat to low and simmer
for about 10 minutes. Serve hot with oyster crackers or
saltines.

SALMON PATTIES

1 Can salmon, drained
3 Tablespoons corn meal
2 Tablespoons flour
Salt and pepper to taste
1 Medium onion, chopped fine
2 Eggs, beaten
Oil for frying

Remove bone and dark skin from salmon. Combine all
ingredients and mix together with hands. Heat oil
(enough to cover halfway up the patty). Pinch off
enough salmon mixture to form a ball. Flatten into patty.
Place in hot oil and fry about 6-8 minutes on each side or
until golden brown. Remove from oil and drain on paper
towels.

SHRIMP AND CRAB CASSEROLE

2 Cups cooked rice
1 Cup salad shrimp
1 Cup crab meat
1/2 Cup chopped onion
1/2 Cup chopped green pepper
1 Can cream of mushroom soup
1/2 Cup milk
1 Cup mayonnaise
4 Tablespoons butter

Saute chopped vegetables in butter. To this, add soup, shrimp and crab. Add milk and mayonnaise and mix thoroughly. Spread rice into a large casserole dish that has been sprayed with non-stick oil. Cover with seafood mixture and bake in 350-degree oven until nicely browned.

GARLIC SHRIMP

1 1/2 Pounds shrimp
1 Cup butter
1 Garlic clove, chopped fine

Remove shell and de-vein shrimp; wash thoroughly. Drain on paper towels. In a heavy saucepan, melt butter and saute garlic for 2 minutes on medium heat. Add shrimp and continue to cook for 5-7 minutes. Shrimp will turn bright pink when done.

PAUL'S FISH STEW

2 Pounds red snapper
2 medium potatoes, diced
1 Small onion, chopped fine
4 Cups Half and Half
1/4 Teaspoon salt
2 Tablespoons sherry
1/2 Teaspoon seafood seasoning
2 Tablespoons butter
2 Tablespoons Worcestershire sauce

Important: Defrost frozen fish in microwave. When thawed, leave in microwave and cook for 3 minutes on high or until fish turns white. In large saucepan melt butter, add potatoes and onion. Cook until tender on low heat. Pour in milk and add flaked fish, wine, seafood seasoning, Worcestershire sauce and salt. Bring to a low boil on medium heat, stirring well. Reduce heat to simmer and continue to cook for 10-15 minutes.

ROSE'S OYSTER STEW

2 Pounds fresh oysters
2 Tablespoons butter
1 Quart Half and Half
1 Tablespoon seafood seasoning

Melt butter in frying pan and add oysters. Simmer for 3 minutes. In a sauce pan, pour in Half and Half, add seasoning and bring to a boil. Add oysters and butter from frying pan. Reduce heat and simmer for 3 minutes. Serve piping hot with oyster or saltine crackers.

SALMON CROQUETTES

1 Can salmon
1 Cup white sauce (to follow)
1 Teaspoon lemon juice
Salt and pepper to taste
1 Large egg, beaten
Bread crumbs for rolling

Drain salmon. Remove skin and bones. Break into small pieces but don't mash. Combine salmon, lemon juice, salt, pepper and hot white sauce and turn out onto a plate to cool. When cold, shape into croquettes about 2 1/2" long. Roll in bread crumbs, dip in egg and roll in crumbs again. Fry in deep fat until nicely brown. Drain on paper towels.

WHITE SAUCE

2 1/2 Tablespoons butter
1/3 Cup flour
1 Cup milk
1/4 Teaspoon salt
1/8 Teaspoon pepper

Combine flour, salt and pepper. Melt butter. When hot and bubbly, add flour mixture. Stir until smooth. Add milk gradually and cook for 20 minutes. This sauce is excellent with any kind of vegetable.

SHRIMP GUMBO

3 Tablespoons butter
1 Pound okra, sliced
3 Tablespoon flour
1 Pound ham
1 Large onion
1 Large bell pepper
1 Can tomato paste

3 Cups water
1 1/2 Teaspoons tabas-
co sauce
2 Pounds cleaned
shrimp
Salt and pepper to
taste

Brown okra in butter until light brown. Remove okra from butter and stir in flour, salt and pepper; stir until brown. Pour in enough water to make a thick gravy; pour into okra. Dice ham, onion and pepper; add to pot along with tomato paste and 3 cups of water. Cover and reduce heat. Cook slowly for 1 1/2 hours. Add shrimp; cook for additional 15minutes.

CATFISH STEW

1 1/2 Pounds catfish fillets
1 Pound bacon
1 1/2 Cups chopped onion
4 Cups diced potatoes
2 Cans tomatoes

1/3 Cup tomato paste
2 Tablespoons Worces-
tershire sauce
Salt and pepper to
taste

Fry bacon until crispy. While bacon is frying, cut fillets into bite-size pieces. Remove bacon and place on paper towels to drain. Fry fish and onion in bacon grease until fish are done and onion is tender; set aside. In a large pot, combine other ingredients and bring to a boil. Cover, reduce heat and simmer until potatoes are tender. Pour fish, onions and bacon grease into boiling mixture. Cover and simmer 20 minutes more.

SOUTHERN FRIED CRAPPIE OR BREAM

Step 1: First, catch the fish (hand size if you're lucky)

Step 2: Scale the fish with a scaler. Remove head. Split belly and remove innards.

Step 3: Rinse thoroughly, inside and out. Place the fish in a pan of cold water until ready to bread. Leave wet so cornmeal will adhere.

Step 4: Pour 2-3 inches of oil in fish pan (enough to cover fish). Place on a propane burner (outside) and allow oil to heat while breading fish.

Step 5: In a poke (a bag) pour cornmeal (how much depends on how lucky you were) along with salt and pepper to your liking and shake to mix. Place fish in bag, a few at a time. Shake to coat.

Step 6: Carefully drop fish into hot oil, don't overcrowd. Fish will float when done and will be a dark golden brown.

Step 7: Remove from oil; drain on paper towels or paper bags.

Step 8: Enjoy!

These are delicious with fried sweet potatoes, rice or grits, cole slaw and hushpuppies.

SHRIMP KABOB

2 Pounds shrimp
1 Green pepper
1 Red pepper
1 Medium onion
1/4 Cup butter
1/2 Teaspoon cream of tartar
1 Lemon, sliced
1 Teaspoon Worcestershire sauce
1/2 Teaspoon red ground pepper
1/2 Teaspoon ground garlic

Cut vegetables into 1" pieces. Steam peppers for about 5 minutes before placing on skewers. Remove shell and de-vein shrimp. Place on skewer in this order: 1 shrimp, 1 piece green pepper, 1 piece onion, 1 piece red pepper. Repeat procedure, leaving about 2 inches at end of skewer. Prepare basting sauce by melting butter . Add Worcestershire sauce, red ground pepper, cream of tartar and ground garlic. Squeeze lemon juice in and mix well. Place kabob on the grill and baste with sauce.

SWEET AND SOUR SHRIMP

2 Tablespoons cornstarch
3 Tablespoons sugar
1 Cup chicken broth
2/3 Cup pineapple juice
4 Tablespoons vinegar
5 Teaspoons soy sauce
1 Tablespoon butter
2 Cups shrimp,
  cleaned

In heavy saucepan, combine cornstarch and sugar; stir in broth. Add pineapple juice, vinegar, soy sauce and butter. Bring to a boil. Add shrimp, cover and simmer for 5-7 minutes or until shrimp are done. Excellent served over white rice.

CODFISH LOAF

1 cup milk
1 cup soft bread crumbs
2 cups cooked codfish
Grated rind of one lemon
1 teaspoon salt
Pepper to taste
2 tablespoons butter
2 eggs, beaten

Scald milk and pour over bread crumbs, allowing to soak until crumbs have absorbed most of it. Combine this with fish, lemon rind, seasonings and melted butter. Fold in eggs. Pour into well-greased loaf pan. Place in a pan of water and bake in a 350-degree oven for 45 minutes. Serve hot with shrimp sauce.

Shrimp sauce:
3 tablespoons butter
3 tablespoons flour
1/2 teaspoon salt
1/4 teaspoon paprika
1/2 cup cooked, shredded shrimp
1 1/2 cups milk

Melt butter add flour and paprika. Stir until you have a smooth paste. Pour in milk slowly and stir until thickened. Add shrimp and bring to a boil. Remove from heat and serve at once.

JIMMY'S LOW COUNTRY BOIL

1/2 Bushel crabs, cleaned
5 Lbs.. Large shrimp, unpeeled
3 Pounds smoked sausage
2 or 3 Large onions, peeled and quartered
5 Pounds. White potatoes, unpeeled
12 Ears corn on cob
Salt and pepper to taste

You will need a large cooking pot with a basket so ingredients can be lifted out of water and drained. Slice sausage into 1-inch pieces. Shuck and clean corn and cut each ear into 2 pieces. Combine ingredients and cover with water. Bring to a boil and cook for about 30 minutes. Lift from water and drain.

This is Sharon's husband, Jimmy's, recipe. He loves to cook and experiment with different dishes, and usually prepares this meal when there is a large crowd over. He always cooks it outside on a gas burner. When cooked and drained, he dumps it out of the basket onto the table that has a thick covering of newspaper, and everyone digs in. It makes for a festive occasion.

BREADS

SOUTHERN LADIES
KNOW HOW TO COOK IT!

FAMILY
FAVORITES

GOD'S PAINTBRUSH

I see the sunbeams streaming down.
God's infinite beauty is all around.
It's as if He pulled a brush from out
of the air,
and painted pictures everywhere.
Man's tried to duplicate this with
canvas and paint,
to paint pictures like God, they
come close but can't.
Bring out the colors and all the deep
hues, of the dusky red roses or the
crystal clear dew.
To capture the beauty of birds on wing,
their work is lovely to look at but
something's missing it seems.
So as you walk across His canvas,
take your time don't rush.
Stop and admire the beauty of what
He's done with His paint brush!

Copyright 1997
Sharon A. Strickland

CORNBREAD AND SWEET MILK

Big hunk corn bread
Whole milk

In a tall glass, crumble cornbread, crust too, about 3/4 full. Pour milk over to cover. Eat with a spoon.

CORNBREAD AND BUTTERMILK

Fill a tall glass 2/3 full with crumbled cornbread. Chop a bit of mild onion on top. Cover with buttermilk. Eat with a spoon and enjoy!

BROWN SUGAR TOAST

Melt 2 tablespoons butter in a skillet. When hot, drop 2 slices of bread in turning quickly to coat. Fry until golden brown on each side. Remove onto a plate and sprinkle while hot with brown sugar to taste. Pour cold milk over as you would syrup.

CHEESE BISCUITS

2 Cups flour
1/4 Cup shortening
1 Teaspoon salt
1 Cup Cheddar cheese, shredded
2 Teaspoons baking powder
2/3 Cup milk

Combine dry ingredients. Cut in shortening, add milk and knead. Add cheese and continue to knead just until cheese is mixed in. Turn out on floured board and fold. Roll out until about 1/2 inch thick. Cut with floured biscuit cutter. Bake at 450 degrees about 15 minutes or until golden brown.

HUSH PUPPIES

2 Cups corn meal
2 Tablespoons flour
1 Tablespoon baking powder
1 Teaspoon soda
1 Teaspoon salt
1 Medium onion, chopped fine
1 3/4 Cups buttermilk
1 Large egg

Mix dry ingredients. Add egg, stir in onion and milk that have been beaten together. Drop by spoonfuls into hot fat. Puppies will float when done. Drain on paper towels and serve hot.

BAKING POWDER BISCUITS

2 Cups flour
2/3 Cups milk
4 Teaspoons baking powder
1/2 Teaspoon salt
2 Teaspoons sugar
1/2 Teaspoon cream of tartar
1/2 Cup shortening

Combine dry ingredients. Make a hob in center and add shortening and milk. Knead. Turn onto floured pastry board and fold over 5 or 6 times. Roll out and cut with floured biscuit cutter. Bake in a 450-degree oven until nicely browned.

PUMPKIN BREAD

3 Cups flour
1 Teaspoon soda
1 Teaspoon salt
1 Teaspoon cinnamon
2 Cups sugar
2 Cups pumpkin
4 Eggs
1 1/2 Cups vegetable oil
1 Cup chopped nuts

Mix dry ingredients in large bowl. Make a hob in center and add the rest of ingredients. Stir until damp. Pour into loaf pan and bake at 350 degrees for 1 hour.

CORNMEAL MUFFINS

1 Cup yellow corn meal
1 Cup flour
1/4 Cup sugar
2 Teaspoons baking powder
3/4 Teaspoon salt
2 Eggs, slightly beaten
1 Cup buttermilk
1/4 Cup melted shortening

Combine all dry ingredients, mixing well. Add wet ingredients to dry mixture. Mix thoroughly. Pour into greased 12-muffin tin. Bake at 425 degrees for 20-25 minutes or until golden brown.

CORN BREAD FLITTERS

1 Cup cornmeal
2 Tablespoons bacon grease
1 Tablespoon sugar
1/2 Teaspoon salt
Boiling water

Combine ingredients, mixing well. Pour in enough boiling water to make a batter, stirring well. Drop into hot fat by large spoonfuls and fry like pancakes. Brown on both sides. Drain on paper towels. Serve hot.

BUTTERMILK BISCUITS

2 Cups self-rising flour
2/3 Cup buttermilk
1/2 Cup shortening

Cut shortening into flour, add milk and mix with hand until a soft dough forms. Turn out onto heavy floured board and knead for about 30 seconds. Roll out until about 1/2-inch thick and cut with a floured biscuit cutter. Place in a greased baking pan and bake at 475 degrees for about 15 minutes or until nicely browned. Remove from oven and cover with clean hand towel.

CORN BREAD

4 Cups self-rising corn meal
1 Cup self-rising flour
1/3 Cup sugar
1/3 Cup corn oil
2 Eggs
2 Cups buttermilk

Combine ingredients, mixing well. Pour into greased pan. Bake at 450 degrees for about 30 minutes or until golden brown.

SPOON BREAD

2/3 Cup milk
2 Cups corn meal self rising
1/2 Cup sugar

2 Tablespoons butter
4 Eggs
1 Teaspoon salt

Heat milk. Mix dry ingredients and add eggs and butter. Add milk and mix thoroughly. Pour into greased glass baking dish and bake for 1 hour in 350-degree oven.

DATE BREAD

1 Cup dates, chopped
1 Cup boiling water
1/2 Teaspoon soda

Sprinkle soda over dates. Pour water over dates and let stand while mixing the following:

1 Cup brown sugar
4 Tablespoons butter
1/2 Teaspoon salt
2 Eggs, beaten

1 1/2 Cups flour
1 Teaspoon baking powder
1 Cup walnuts, chopped
fine

Combine ingredients, including date mixture, mixing well. Pour into prepared loaf pan. Bake at 350 degrees for 50 minutes to 1 hour. Cool before slicing.

COFFEE BREAD

1 1/2 Cups flour
3 Tablespoons sugar
2 Teaspoons baking powder
4 Tablespoons shortening

1 Egg
1/4 Teaspoon salt
1/2 Cup milk

Mix flour, baking powder, sugar and salt. Cut in shortening. Add egg and milk to make a soft dough. Turn into shallow buttered pan and push to edges. Cover with topping that follows

Topping:
2/3 Cup brown sugar
1/3 Cup chopped pecans

1 Teaspoon cinnamon
3 Tablespoons soft butter

Mix ingredients until crumbly. Sprinkle over dough. Bake at 350 degrees for 20 minutes. When almost cooled, cut into bars.

CRACKLIN' CORNBREAD

3 cups cornmeal
2 cups cracklin's
1 1/2 teaspoons baking powder
2 cups buttermilk
1/2 cup water
1 egg, slightly beaten
1 teaspoon salt

Mix dry ingredients. Add buttermilk, water and egg, stirring well; fold in the cracklin's. Bake at 475 degrees until golden brown.

CORNMEAL MUSH

1 cup cornmeal
1 teaspoon salt
1 quart water

Bring water and salt to a boil. Slowly stir in cornmeal and reduce heat. Cook until thickened like grits. Serve as a hot cereal with butter, sugar and milk.

CORNMEAL BISCUITS

1 cup yellow cornmeal   3/4 cup buttermilk
3/4 cup flour   1/4 cup shortening
3/4 teaspoon salt
4 teaspoons baking powder

Mix dry ingredients. Add buttermilk and shortening to make soft dough. Roll out on floured board and cut with biscuit cutter. Bake at 450 degrees for about 20 minutes or until nicely browned.

ORANGE CINNAMON ROLLS

Dough:
2 Cups flour
3 Teaspoons baking powder
1 Teaspoon salt
6 Tablespoons shortening
2/3 Cup buttermilk

Filling:
3 Tablespoons melted butter
1/3 Cup dark brown sugar
1 1/2 Teaspoons cinnamon
1 Tablespoon grated orange rind
1/4 Cup chopped pecans

Sift together flour, baking powder and salt. Cut in shortening and add milk to form a soft dough. Knead as you would for biscuits. Turn out onto a floured pastry board and roll out thin to make a triangle. Pour butter onto dough and spread to edges. Sprinkle on brown sugar, cinnamon, orange rind and pecans. Roll up into tight log and seal edge with fingers. With serrated knife, cut into 1" slices. Place on greased cookie sheet and bake for 15-17 minutes. Glaze while warm.

Glaze:
3/4 Cup hot water
1 Tablespoon shortening
1 Tablespoon unflavored gelatin
1 1/2 boxes 4X sugar
1 Teaspoon orange flavoring

Soak gelatin in 3 tablespoons water. Melt shortening in hot water. Add gelatin, then sugar and orange flavoring, beating until smooth. Pour over warm rolls.

HEALTH BREAD

2 Cups whole wheat flour
3/4 Teaspoon salt
4 Teaspoons baking powder
2 Teaspoons shortening
1 Cup milk
1/4 Cup chopped raisins

Mix flour, salt and baking powder well. Cut in shortening; until coarsely fine. Add raisins and milk to make a soft dough. Drop by tablespoon into greased muffin tins. Bake at 350 degrees for 25-30 minutes.

BANANA FRITTERS

1 Cup flour
2 Teaspoons baking powder
1 Tablespoon powdered sugar
1/4 Teaspoon salt
1 Egg, beaten
1/4 Cup milk
1 Tablespoon lemon juice
3 Bananas, mashed fine

Combine dry ingredients and sift. Add others in order listed, except bananas. Force bananas through a sieve before adding to batter; beat thoroughly. Drop by spoonfuls into hot oil. Fry until golden brown. Drain on paper towels. Sprinkle with powdered sugar.

CORN AND RICE PONE

2 Cups cornmeal
5 Teaspoons baking powder
1 Teaspoon salt
2 Tablespoons sugar
3 Eggs, beaten
2 1/4 Cups milk
1/4 Cup melted shortening
1 Cup cooked rice

Combine and sift dry ingredients; add milk and shortening to beaten eggs. Stir into dry ingredients. Mix in rice and pour into greased baking pans. Bake at 450 degrees for 30 minutes or until nicely brown.

PEANUT BUTTER BREAD

2 Cups flour
4 Teaspoons baking powder
1 Teaspoon salt
1/2 Cup sugar
2/3 Cup peanut butter
1 Cup milk

Sift together flour, salt, baking powder and sugar. Add milk to peanut butter, blending well. Add to dry ingredients and beat thoroughly. Bake in greased loaf pan at 300 degrees for 45-50 minutes. Better if made the day before use.

Helpful hint: In substituting brown sugar for granulated white sugar, it is best to use weight for weight rather than measure for measure.

ZUCCHINI NUT CARROT BREAD

1 Cup oil
3/4 Cup sugar
1/2 Cup brown sugar
1 Teaspoon vanilla
2 Eggs
2 Cups flour
1 Teaspoon cinnamon
1 Teaspoon nutmeg
1 Teaspoon salt
1 Teaspoon soda
1 Cup instant potato flakes
1/2 Teaspoon baking powder
1/2-3/4 Cup buttermilk
1 Cup grated zucchini
1 Cup grated carrots
1 Cup broken English walnut pieces

Beat together oil, white sugar, brown sugar, vanilla and eggs. Combine flour, salt, soda, baking powder, spices and potato flakes; mix well. Add to oil mixture, alternately with buttermilk, beating until well blended. Stir in zucchini carrot and nuts. Pour into well-greased and floured loaf pan. Bake at 350 degrees for 45 minutes to one hour, checking at 45 minutes.

COFFEE CAN BREAD

3 1/4 cups plain flour
1/2 cup water
1/2 cup oil
4 tablespoons sugar
1 package yeast
2 eggs, room temp., slightly beaten
3/4-1 cup Cheddar cheese, grated
1 teaspoon salt
1/2 cup milk
1 teaspoon of salt

Mix water, oil, sugar and milk; place on heat just to warm. While mixture is heating, combine 1 1/4 cups flour and yeast, beating for 2 minutes. Pour warmed mixture into flour and yeast. Add eggs and cheese, mixing well. Add remaining flour (mixtures should be like elastic). Grease two 1-pound coffee cans, divide mixture and place inside. Allow to rise for one hour in a warm place. Bake at 350 degrees for 25-30 minutes.

REFRIGERATOR YEAST ROLLS

2 Packages dry yeast
2 Cups warm water
1 Cup shortening
1/2 Cup sugar
2 Eggs
6 Cups flour
1 Tablespoon salt

Dissolve yeast in water. In a large mixing bowl, combine shortening, sugar and eggs; beat well. Add water that yeast has been added to, and then flour and salt. Place in greased bowl and let rise overnight in refrigerator. Roll out on floured board and pinch off enough to roll into 1" balls; allow to rise again. Bake at 450 degrees until golden brown.

CORNMEAL CAKE

1 Cup cornmeal
2 Cups flour
1 Cup sugar
3 Tablespoons butter
2 Teaspoons baking powder

1/2 Teaspoon salt
1 Cup milk
2 Eggs

Combine ingredients, mixing well. Pour into greased oblong baking dish Bake at 375 degrees 25-30 minutes.

GINGERBREAD

1/2 Cup butter
1 Cup brown sugar
1 Egg, well beaten
1 Cup molasses

1 Cup buttermilk
1 Teaspoon soda
1 Teaspoon ginger
3 Cups flour

Cream butter and sugar. Add egg and molasses. Stir soda into buttermilk and add to creamed mixture. Combine flour and ginger; mix thoroughly. Add to creamed mixture and mix well. Pour into greased 8"x8"x2" pan. Bake at 350 degrees 30-35 minutes or until done. Serve plain or with lemon butter.

Lemon Butter:
4 Cups sugar
3 Large lemons
6 Eggs, well beaten
1 Stick butter

Grate rinds of lemons, set aside. Squeeze and collect juice. To juice, add sugar, lemon rind and eggs. Cook over low heat, stirring constantly until mixture begins to thicken. Remove from heat and stir in butter. Serve cold with warm gingerbread.

103

PINEAPPLE FRITTERS

Batter:
1 Cup flour
1/4 Teaspoon salt
1 1/2 Teaspoons baking powder
1 Egg, beaten
1/2 Cup milk
1/2 Cup sugar

Pineapple:
1 Can pineapple rings
1 Cup brown sugar

Drain juice from pineapple into a bowl. Mix in brown sugar. Place pineapple in juice and brown sugar. Remove and dip into fritter batter. Fry in deep fat until light brown. Drain on paper towels and sprinkle with powdered sugar. You may use other fruit by chopping and mixing it into batter. Don't chop too fine. Drop by spoonfuls into hot fat. Turning repeatedly until brown on both sides. Drain and sprinkle with powdered sugar.

CAKE DOUGHNUTS

3 Cups flour
2/3 Cup sugar
1 Teaspoon cinnamon
3/4 Teaspoon salt
4 Teaspoons baking powder
3 Tablespoons shortening
1 Egg
2/3 Cup milk

Cream shortening, add sugar and egg, stir in milk Combine cinnamon, salt, baking powder and flour. Mix thoroughly. If dough isn't stiff enough to roll out, add a small amount of flour so it can be. Roll out on a floured board until about 1/4 inch thick. Cut with doughnut cutter and fry in deep hot fat. Drain on paper towels.

YAM NUT MUFFINS

1 1/3 Cups light brown sugar
1/2 Cup shortening
2 Eggs, beaten
1 3/4 Cups flour
1 Teaspoon cinnamon
3/4 Cup buttermilk
1 1/4 Cups mashed yams
1/2 Cup light raisins
1/2 Cup chopped English walnuts

Cream sugar and shortening until fluffy. Combine other ingredients, except raisins and walnuts, mixing well. Stir into sugar mixture. Fold in raisins and chopped nuts. Spray muffin pan with non-stick spray. Fill with batter 2/3 full. Bake at 425 degrees 20-25 or until brown. Baking time varies with size of muffin pans.

SMOKY MOUNTAIN CORNBREAD

1 Cup cornmeal
2 Tablespoons sugar
1/2 Cup flour
2 Eggs, beaten
2 Teaspoons baking powder
1 Cup buttermilk
1 Teaspoon salt
3 Tablespoons bacon grease

Combine dry ingredients, mixing well. Add eggs, buttermilk and grease. Heat skillet on top of stove with a little grease in it. When hot, pour in batter. Remove from stove immediately. Bake in a 450 degree oven for 20-25 minutes or until top is golden brown.

Helpful hint: Cornbread is better baked in a hot oven. 450-475 degrees usually does the trick.

BROCCOLI CORNBREAD

1 12oz. Package frozen broccoli, thawed
1 Large onion, chopped
6oz. Cottage cheese
1 Package cornbread mix
1/2 Cup melted margarine, melted
4 Eggs beaten
1/2 Teaspoon salt

Combine ingredients, mixing well. Turn into a greased 9x13 baking pan. Bake at 400 degrees for 25 minutes or until golden brown.

ORIGINAL HOE CAKE

2 Cups corn meal
1/2 Teaspoon salt
1 Cup boiling water
2 Tablespoon bacon grease

Combine ingredients; mix well. Shape into cake with hands and flatten. Bake on well-greased griddle or iron frying pan on top of stove. Turn once halfway through baking in order for both sides to brown. Cook through.

It is said, workers in the cotton fields cooked this bread on their hoes over an open fire and this is how it got it's name.

OLD TIMEY BLUEBERRY MUFFINS

1/2 Cup shortening
1 Cup sugar
1 Cup flour
2 Teaspoons baking powder
1/2 Teaspoon salt
3 Eggs, beaten
1 Cup milk
1 Teaspoon vanilla
1 Cup fresh blueberries

Cream sugar and shortening until fluffy. Combine flour, salt and baking powder. Add to shortening mixture. Beat together eggs, milk and vanilla. Add to creamed mixture, beating until smooth. Measure 2 tablespoons of flour into a bag. Shake blueberries in flour until lightly covered. Fold into batter. Pour into greased muffin tin, filling each cup 2/3 full. Bake at 400 degrees for 20-25 minutes.

RICE MUFFINS

1 Egg, beaten
1 Teaspoon vanilla
2 Tablespoons Butter, melted
1/2 Cup milk
3/4 Cup cooked rice
1 Cup flour
1/4 Teaspoon salt
1 1/2 Teaspoon baking powder
2 Tablespoons sugar

Mix dry ingredients. Add remainder of ingredients, mixing until just moistened. Fill greased muffin tins 2/3 full and bake at 400 degrees for 25-30 minutes.

"I pray for your
happiness
and a heart
that's light."
— Sharon Strickland

SOUTHERN LADIES
KNOW HOW TO COOK IT!

SOUTHERN
DELIGHTS

CHILD'S PRAYER OF THANKSGIVING

Thank you for a world so sweet.
Thank you for the food we eat.
Thank you for the birds that sing.
Thank you, God, for everything.

RAISIN WHEAT COOKIES

1/2 Cup shortening
1 Cup sugar
1 Teaspoon vanilla
1 3/4 Cups flour
1/4 Teaspoon salt
2 1/2 Teaspoons baking powder
2 Cups puffed wheat
1 Cup raisins
2 eggs, beaten

Cream shortening and sugar. Add eggs that vanilla has been added to. Sift together dry ingredients except puffed wheat. Combine this and shortening mixture. Fold in puffed wheat and raisins. Drop by teaspoon onto greased cookie sheet. Bake at 375 degrees for 8-10 minutes or until done.

OLD FASHIONED RICH SUGAR COOKIES

1 Cup butter
1 1/2 Cups sugar
3 Eggs, beaten
1 Teaspoon vanilla
1/2 Teaspoon almond extract
1/4 Teaspoon salt
1 Teaspoon baking powder
3 1/2 Cups flour
1/2 Cup chopped pecans

Cream butter and sugar until soft. Add eggs, extracts and salt. Beat for another 2 minutes. Add flour and baking powder. Mix just enough for ingredients to hold together. Add nuts. Pinch off small pieces and roll into small balls and place on greased cookie sheet; flatten with spatula. Bake in a 350-degree oven for 8-9 minutes.

CHRISTMAS COOKIES

1 Cup brown sugar
1 Cup white sugar
1 Cup butter
1 Cup shortening
2 Eggs
1 Cup citron
Juice and rind of 1 orange
1 Teaspoon soda
3 Teaspoons water
1 Cup chopped nuts
5 Cups flour
Candied cherry halves

Cream sugars, butter and shortening. Beat in eggs and juice of orange and water. Combine other ingredients and add to creamed mixture. Roll out flat on floured pastry board. Roll up, cover and place in refrigerator until chilled. Slice and press cherry half into each cookie. Place on greased cookie sheet. Bake in a 350-degree oven for 8-10 minutes.

BUTTER CUP BARS

1 Cup butter
2 1/2 Cups graham cracker crumbs
2 1/2 Cups 10X sugar
1 Cup peanut butter
2 Cups butterscotch chips

Melt butter. Add crumbs, peanut butter and sugar mixing well. Spread into a greased oblong pan. Melt butterscotch chips and spread evenly on top of mixture. Chill until firm. Cut into bars.

CHOCOLATE OATMEAL
NO BAKE COOKIES

2 Cups sugar
1/2 Cup cocoa
1/2 Cup milk
1 Stick margarine
3 Cups quick-cook oatmeal
2 Tablespoons peanut butter

Bring sugar, cocoa, milk and margarine to a boil stirring continuously. Take off heat. Add oatmeal and peanut butter, mixing well. Drop by tablespoon onto wax paper.

Can also be placed in bottom of decorative muffin tin liners and given as gifts. This gift, we look forward too each Christmas from Sharon's daughter, Angie. Our sister Melanie started the tradition of giving these, and Angie has carried it on.

CARROT COOKIES

1 Cup hot mashed carrots
1 Cup shortening
3/4 Cup sugar
1 Egg
1 1/2 Teaspoons lemon extract
2 Teaspoon baking powder
1/3 Teaspoon salt
2 Cups flour

Mix carrots and shortening together while carrots are hot. Add other ingredients in order listed, mixing well but not over-beating. Drop by spoonfuls onto cookie sheet and bake 12-15 minutes at 350 degrees.

Moutain Lore & Superstition

"Place blue bottles in the window to ward off bad luck."

GINGER CREAMS

1/2 Cup brown sugar
1/2 Cup shortening
1 Egg, beaten
1/2 Cup molasses
1 Tablespoon ginger
1 Teaspoon soda
3/4 Teaspoon salt
2 1/2 Cups flour

Cream sugar and shortening. Add egg and molasses. Sift ginger, soda, salt and flour together. Gradually add to creamed mixture, mixing well. Pinch off small amounts and roll into balls. Arrange on baking sheet and flatten with spatula. Bake in a 350-degree oven for about 10 minutes or until lightly browned.

DAINTY COOKIES

1 Cup butter
1 Cup sugar
3 Eggs
2 Cups flour
1/2 Cup marmalade

Cream butter and sugar; add eggs mixing well. Gradually add flour. Turn onto pastry board that has been lightly sprinkled with powdered sugar. Roll until very thin. Cut with round cookie cutter. Place one teaspoon of marmalade into center of each cookie. Fold over and crimp edges with a fork. Bake in a 375-degree oven for 8-10 minutes or until delicately browned.

TOASTED COCONUT BALLS

1 Small bag of coconut
1 Box 4X sugar
1 14oz. Can sweetened condensed milk
1 12oz. Package chocolate chips
1/2 Block paraffin wax

Scatter coconut onto large baking sheet. Place in 400-degree oven and toast until golden brown. Remove from oven and cool completely. Mix sugar, condensed milk and coconut. Take mixture out by rounded teaspoonfuls and roll into balls with hands and chill. Place chocolate chips and paraffin wax in top of double boiler. Heat until both have melted. Dip balls into chocolate with toothpick. Place on wax paper-lined cookie sheet and chill.

CHOCOLATE-COVERED CHERRIES

1 Stick butter, softened
1 Tablespoon heavy cream
1 Box 4X sugar
1 Teaspoon vanilla
1 16oz. Jar whole maraschino cherries
1 12oz. Package chocolate chips
1/2 Block paraffin wax

Beat butter, cream, sugar and vanilla just until smooth. Make sure cherries are well drained (I usually drain them on paper towels). Pinch off just enough sugar mixture to mold around each cherry. Melt chocolate chips and paraffin in top of double boiler until melted. Dip each cherry into the chocolate with a toothpick. Place on wax paper to cool.

CHOCOLATE-COVERED
PEANUT CLUSTERS

3 Cups semi-sweet chocolate chips
4 Cups roasted peanuts

Melt chocolate in top of double boilers. Add peanuts and stir. Drop by tablespoons onto wax paper and allow to cool.

SPICED PECANS

2 Cups pecan halves
2 Tablespoons butter, melted
1 1/2 Cups 4X sugar
1/8 Teaspoon salt
2 Teaspoons cinnamon
1/2 Teaspoon nutmeg

Stir pecans into butter and spread on cookie sheet. Bake at 350 degrees for 8-10 minutes, stirring frequently. Combine sugar, salt and spices into a bag. Shake well. Add pecans and shake to coat. Remove pecans and shake off excess sugar mixture. Store in airtight container.

PECAN LOGS

1 Pound confectioners sugar
1 7oz. Jar marshmallow creme
2 Teaspoons vanilla
1 14oz. Package caramels
1/3 Cup evaporated milk
Chopped pecans for rolling

Combine sugar, marshmallow creme and vanilla, mixing well. Shape into 3 or 4 logs and place on wax paper. Melt caramel in milk in top of double boiler, stirring occasionally. Spoon over logs. When slightly cooled, roll in pecans to coat. When completely cooled, cut into slices.

CHOCOLATE-DIPPED STRAWBERRIES

1 6oz Package semi-sweet chocolate chips
1 Pint fresh strawberries with caps and stems

Melt chocolate in top of double boiler. Rinse strawberries and dry completely. Dip each berry, holding by stem into chocolate until bottom half is covered. Place on wax paper until chocolate is set.

BUTTER CREAM BALLS

4 Squares semi-sweet chocolate
1/2 Cup butter
2 Cups sifted confectioners sugar
1 Teaspoon vanilla
Ground toasted pecans for rolling

Melt chocolate and butter in top of double boiler, stirring occasionally. Cool. Stir in sugar, mixing well. Stir in vanilla. Cool until firm. Shape into 1" balls and insert toothpick. Dip into chocolate. Roll in ground pecans. Place in foil bonbon cups. Makes a beautiful homemade Christmas gift.

CREAMY MINTS

4 oz. Cream cheese
1/2 Teaspoon oil of peppermint
Choice of food color
3 1/3 Cups confectioners sugar

Blend cream cheese, peppermint oil and food color. Add confectioners sugar and knead until well mixed. Shape into marble-sized balls. Press into candy molds sprayed with non-stick spray.

COCONUT MACAROONS

1 Large bag coconut
1 Teaspoon vanilla
1 Can sweetened condensed milk
Maraschino cherries

Combine all ingredients and mix well. Drop by spoonfuls onto greased cookie sheet. Press half of a maraschino cherry onto each cookie. Bake in a 350 degree oven for 8-10 minutes. Remove immediately from pan. When cool, store in airtight container.

NO-BAKE COOKIES

1/2 Cup sugar
1/2 Cup white corn syrup
1/2 Cup peanut butter (crunchy)
1 Cup corn flakes
1 Teaspoon vanilla

Combine sugar and corn syrup; bring to a boil in heavy sauce pan. Blend peanut butter, cereal and vanilla; add to syrup mixture. Drop by spoonfuls onto greased cookie sheet. Cover with wax paper and refrigerate.

NO-BAKE ORANGE BALLS

1 7oz. Box vanilla wafers, crushed
1/2 Cup orange juice concentrate
3/4 Cup powdered sugar
3/4 Cup flaked coconut

Mix ingredients and roll into small balls. Roll in powdered sugar. Store in airtight container.

BUTTERSCOTCH BALLS

2 Sticks butter
2 2/3 Cups graham cracker crumbs
1 Cup chopped pecans
1 Can flaked coconut
3/4 Cup peanut butter
1 Box 4X sugar
1 Tablespoon vanilla
1 Pack butterscotch chips
1/2 Stick paraffin wax

Melt butter. Add crumbs, pecans, coconut, peanut butter, sugar, and vanilla. Mix well. Roll into balls about the size of a large marble. Melt butterscotch chips and paraffin wax in top of double boiler. Insert toothpick into each ball and dip into butterscotch mixture. Place on wax paper. Keep butterscotch warm until all balls have been dipped.

MOUNDS

1 Can sweetened condensed milk
1 Stick margarine, softened
2 Boxes powdered sugar
2 Cups coconut
1/2 Stick paraffin wax
1 1/2 Bags chocolate chips

Mix condensed milk and margarine. Add sugar and coconut. Roll into small balls. Melt chocolate chips and wax in top of double boiler. With toothpick, dip each ball in melted chocolate. Cool on wax paper.

HARD CANDY

4 Cups sugar
1 Cup white corn syrup
1 Cup water
1 Teaspoon flavored oil, your choice, not flavoring
Choice of food coloring

Dust 2 large cookie pans with powdered sugar and set aside. Combine sugar, syrup and water in heavy sauce pan. Stir until sugar is dissolved. Boil until candy thermometer reaches 290 degrees over high heat (about 20-25 minutes). Remove from heat and add oils and food coloring. Stir to mix. Pour onto cookie sheets and cool. When completely cooled, break into bite-size pieces. Store in airtight container.

CHOCOLATE COCONUT DROPS

1 1/2 Cups flaked coconut
1 Cup marshmallow cream
1/8 Teaspoon salt
1/2 Teaspoon vanilla
1- 4 1/2oz. Chocolate candy bar

Place coconut in thin layer on a baking sheet. Toast in 400-degree oven until light brown. Mix together marshmallow cream, salt, coconut and vanilla. Stir until well blended. Roll into small balls and refrigerate while melting candy bar. Melt candy bar over low heat in a heavy sauce pan. With a toothpick, dip each ball into chocolate. Place on wax paper and chill.

BOURBON BALLS

5 Squares chocolate
1/2 Cup chopped pecans
1/2 Cup margarine
1 Pound powdered sugar
6 Tablespoons bourbon
1/3 Cup paraffin wax

Soak pecans overnight in bourbon. Cream margarine and sugar well. Stir in nuts and bourbon. Shape into balls. Chill while melting chocolate and paraffin in top of double boiler. With toothpick, dip each ball into chocolate. Chill on wax paper.

EASY FUDGE

2/3 Cup evaporated milk
1 2/3 Cups sugar
1 1/2 Cups miniature marshmallows
1/2 Cup chopped walnuts
1 1/2 Cups semi sweet chocolate pieces
1 Teaspoon vanilla

Stir milk and sugar in heavy saucepan. Over medium heat, bring to a boil, stirring constantly. Cook 5 minutes. Remove from heat and stir in remaining ingredients. Stir until chocolate and marshmallows are melted. Pour into an 8x8" pan that has been sprayed with non-stick spray or oiled. Cool completely before cutting into squares.

OLD TIMEY PEANUT BRITTLE

2 Cups roasted peanuts
3 Cups sugar

Pour sugar into frying pan. Stir over medium to medium low heat. The sugar will lump and will eventually melt. When melted, and a very light brown, pour in peanuts and stir. Pour quickly onto a sprayed or greased pan. A non-stick pan works great. Break into small pieces when completely cooled.

CREAM CHEESE FUDGE

2 3oz. Packs cream cheese
4 Cups powdered sugar
4 1oz. Squares unsweetened chocolate, melted
1/2 Teaspoon vanilla
3/4 Cup pecans, chopped
1/8 Teaspoon salt

Bring cream cheese to room temperature. Beat until smooth. Slowly add sugar. Add melted chocolate, mixing well. Stir in vanilla, salt and pecans. Press into sprayed or greased 8x8x2 pan. Chill. When firm, cut into 1-inch squares.

CHOCOLATE COVERED MARSHMALLOWS

8oz. Semi-sweet chocolate
2 Teaspoons shortening
25-30 Large marshmallows

Melt chocolate and shortening in top of double boiler; stir well. Cool slightly before dipping marshmallows or they will melt. Insert toothpick into each marshmallow and dip into chocolate, covering completely. Place on waxed paper and allow to harden before removing from paper. Dip twice for thicker coat.

CARAMEL NUT MARSHMALLOWS

1/2 Pound caramels
2 Tablespoons hot water
16 Large marshmallows
1 Cup chopped peanuts

Melt caramels in hot water in top of double boiler. Stir frequently until candy is melted and smooth. Insert toothpick into marshmallows and dip in hot sauce, covering completely. Don't allow sauce to cool or it will become too stiff. Roll each marshmallow in peanuts. Place on waxed paper to cool.

BUTTERNUT CANDY

1 Cup hot mashed potatoes
3 Boxes 4X sugar
2 Tablespoon margarine
1 Cup toasted coconut
1 Cup chopped pecans
1 Teaspoon butternut flavor
4 Squares chocolate
1/2 Cake paraffin wax

Add sugar to potatoes. Combine coconut, nuts, margarine, and butternut flavoring. Add to potato mixture and mix well. Roll into balls size of large marbles. Melt chocolate and wax in heavy saucepan or top of double boiler. With toothpick, dip each ball into the chocolate. Place on wax paper.

POTATO CANDY

1 Small baked potato
Powdered sugar
Creamy peanut butter
1 Teaspoon milk

Peel potato while hot (potato must be small) and mash thoroughly. Add sugar and milk, a few drops at a time, until a soft dough forms. Pinch off enough dough and form a square shape. Roll out flat on wax paper. Spread thin coat of peanut butter on top of layer. Roll up jelly roll style. Wrap in wax paper and refrigerate until chilled. Repeat procedure until all dough is used. When chilled, slice into 1/2 inch slices. Makes a nice homemade Christmas gift. Place in layer in tins, separating each layer with wax paper.

SCHOOL HOUSE
PEANUT BUTTER COOKIES

1 Cup shortening
1 Cup peanut butter
1 Cup white sugar
1 Cup firmly packed brown sugar
2 Eggs
2 1/2 Cups self rising flour
1 Teaspoon vanilla
1 Teaspoon salt

Cream shortening, peanut butter, white and brown sugar. Add eggs, flour, salt and vanilla; mix well. Pinch off enough dough to make a 1" ball. Place on sprayed cookie sheet and flatten with a fork, making crisscross designs. Bake in 400-degree oven for 8-10 minutes.

BUTTERSCOTCH COOKIES

1 Stick butter
2 Cups firmly packed brown sugar
3 Eggs
1 1/2 Cups flour
1 Tablespoon baking powder
1 Cup pecans, chopped fine
1 Teaspoon vanilla

Cream butter and sugar; add eggs one at a time, beating after each addition. Sift together the flour and baking powder. Add to butter mixture a little at a time. Stir in nuts and vanilla. Spread on a greased and floured baking pan and bake at 325 degrees for 30 minutes. Cool before cutting into squares.

OLD FASHION SOFT COOKIES

1/2 Cup shortening
1/2 Cup sugar
1/2 Cup molasses
1 Egg
2 Teaspoons baking powder
1/2 Teaspoon salt
2 Cups sifted flour
1/2 Cup milk

Cream shortening. Slowly add sugar and beat well. Beat in molasses. Add egg. Sift together dry ingredients and add to creamed mixture alternately with milk. Drop from teaspoon onto greased cookie sheet. Bake at 350 degrees 8-10 minutes or until brown around the edges.

CRISP MOLASSES COOKIES

1/2 Cup butter
1/2 Cup sugar
1/2 Teaspoon salt
1 Teaspoon ginger
1/2 Teaspoon cinnamon
1/4 Teaspoon cloves
1/4 Teaspoon nutmeg
1 Teaspoon soda
1 Egg, unbeaten
1/2 Cup molasses
2 Cups sifted flour

Cream butter and sugar. Add spices and then egg, beating well. Add molasses. Sift flour, salt and soda together and add to creamed mixture. Drop by teaspoons onto greased cookie sheet. Flatten with a glass that has been rolled in sugar. Bake at 350 degrees for 12-15 minutes.

BUTTER COOKIES

1 Cup butter
1 Cup sugar
1 Egg
1 Tablespoon milk
1/2 Teaspoon vanilla
2 3/4 Cups flour
1 Teaspoon baking powder
1/3 Teaspoon salt

Cream butter and sugar. Beat in egg, milk and vanilla. Add dry ingredients and mix well. Chill. Roll out dough until about 1/8" thick and cut with cookie cutter. Place on cookie sheet that has been sprayed with non-stick spray. Bake in a 350-degree oven for 10 minutes.

CHOCOLATE CHIP BARS

1 Cup graham cracker crumbs
1/2 Cup melted butter
1 Cup coconut
1 Cup chocolate chips
1 Cup chopped nuts
1 Can sweetened condensed milk

Combine cracker crumbs, butter, and coconut. Press into oblong baking pan. Sprinkle with chocolate chips then nuts. Pour condensed milk evenly over top. Bake at 350 degrees for 30 minutes.

CAKES & PIES

MEMORIES

As time goes on, and we all will agree,
It will wait for no one, not you nor me;

But it's not time we are counting,
It's good things in between,
The good times we've had,
And the wonders we've seen.

The loved ones God loaned us,
We've shared from the start,
The friends we've made;
A piece of our heart.

So march on, time,
As we know you will,
But leave us our memories,
And the love we feel.

The love for each other,
Family and friends,
Are memories we've made,
That will last to the end.

Rosemary Arrington Newman

SISTERS

Sisters are forever, a bond is formed
from the very start.
A treasured piece of work of art they carry
in their hearts.
Happily embracing life together as they
walk through hand in hand.
their problems and cares in life each
other understands.

God gives us many blessings and
I appreciate each one.
I often stop and pause awhile to
marvel at what He's done.
He gives us friends and family in
this life to help us through.
He must have loved me an awful
lot to give me a sister like you.

Sharon A. Strickland

COCONUT CREAM PIE

2/3 Cup sugar
1/4 Teaspoon salt
1/4 Cup cornstarch
2 Cups milk
3 Egg, separated
2 Tablespoons butter
1 Teaspoon vanilla
1 Cup moist coconut

Scald milk. Combine sugar, cornstarch and salt. Slowly add to milk. Cook over medium heat, stirring constantly until mixture thickens and boils. Cook 2 minutes and remove from heat. Mix small amount of hot mixture into yolks. Add to remaining mixture and cook 1 minute, stirring constantly. Add butter and vanilla. Fold in coconut. Cool about 5 minutes, stirring twice. Pour into baked pastry shell. Cover with meringue topping and bake at 350 degrees for about 15 minutes or until a delicate brown. Cool before refrigerating.

GEORGIA COCONUT PIE

2 Cups sugar
1 Stick margarine, melted
4 Eggs
2 Heaping tablespoons flour
1 Cup milk
2 1/3 Cups coconut
2 1/2 Teaspoons vanilla

Mix first 5 ingredients. Add coconut and vanilla. Pour into 2 unbaked pie shells and bake in 450-degree oven for 10 minutes. Reduce heat to 375 degrees and bake about 25 minutes or until filling is set. Cool on wire racks.

BASIC PIE PASTRY

1 1/2 Cups sifted flour
1/2 Teaspoon salt
1/2 Cup shortening
4-5 Tablespoons ice water

Sift together flour and salt. Cut in shortening with pastry blender until pieces are size of small peas. Sprinkle water, a tablespoon at a time, over mix. Mix with a fork. Form a ball with your hands and set aside for a few minutes. Flour pastry board. Place half of dough on board and flatten. Roll out to fit pan. This recipe makes enough dough for two single crusts or one double crust.

BASIC MERINGUE

3 Egg whites
1/4 Teaspoon cream of tartar
6 Tablespoons sugar

Beat whites and cream of tartar until frothy. Beat in sugar, 1 tablespoon at a time until meringue is stiff and has a gloss. Beat until stiff enough to hold a point but still with a gloss. Don't overbeat.

SOUTHERN PECAN PIE

9 Eggs
3 Cups sugar
1 Cup butter
1 Teaspoon vanilla
3/4 Teaspoon salt
1 1/2 Cups white corn syrup
3 Cups pecans

Combine ingredients and pour into unbaked pie shells. Bake at 350 degrees for 45-50 minutes. Makes 2 or 3 pies depending on size of shells.

CHOCOLATE PECAN PIE

2 Eggs
1 Cup sugar
1/2 Cup flour
1 Stick margarine, melted
1 Teaspoon vanilla
1 Cup coarsely chopped pecans
1 6oz. Package semi-sweet chocolate

Beat eggs slightly in a medium bowl. Blend in sugar, flour, melted margarine, and vanilla. Stir in pecans and chocolate pieces. Pour into unbaked pie shell and bake at 325 degrees for 50 minutes.

YOU NAME IT

1 Large envelope brownie mix complete (just add
   water)
3 3oz. Packages cream cheese, softened
1 3/4 Cups 4X sugar
1 Teaspoon vanilla
1 Stick butter, softened
1 8oz. Carton whipped topping
1/2-1 Cup toasted coconut
12 Maraschino cherries
1/2 Cup toasted pecans

Prepare brownie mix and bake in 9x13 pan according
to package directions Remove from oven and cool completely. In a large bowl, combine cheese and butter.
Cream until light and fluffy. Add vanilla and sugar, con-
tinuing to beat for 2 minutes more. Spread cheese mixture over brownies followed by whipped topping; then
nuts. Sprinkle on toasted coconut and garnish with
whole maraschino cherries. Refrigerate 2-3 hours. Cut
into squares. This is a very rich desert, but oh so easy!

BLUEBERRY BREEZE

1 Small box vanilla instant pudding
1 21oz Can blueberry pie filling
1 8oz. Carton whipped topping
1 Baked or graham cracker crust

Mix pudding according to package directions. Chill
until set. By hand, beat into pudding 1 1/2 cups of
whipped topping just until blended. Fold in blueberry pie
filling. Cover with remainder of whipped topping. Garnish with fresh blueberries.

APRICOT AND NUT ICE CREAM PIE

Crust:
1 1/2 Cups vanilla wafer crumbs
6 Tablespoons margarine
Combine ingredients and press into a 9" pie pan.
Refrigerate until chilled.

Filling:
1 Cup chopped dried apricots
1/2 Cup water
1/2 Cup sugar
1 Tablespoon lemon juice
2/3 Cup chopped walnuts
1 Quart vanilla ice cream, softened

Combine apricots, sugar and water in saucepan.
Bring to a boil; reduce heat and simmer 5 minutes. Add
lemon juice and walnuts. Refrigerate until chilled.
Spread half of chilled mixture onto bottom of crust.
Cover with half of ice cream. Place in freezer. Spread
remaining apricot mixture on top of ice cream layer followed by ice cream. Remove from freezer 5 minutes
before serving.

MINCE MEAT CREAM PIE

1 1/2 Cups mincemeat
2 Teaspoons grated orange peel
1 1/2 Cups milk
1 Small package vanilla instant pudding
1 Baked 8" pie shell

Spread mincemeat on bottom of pie shell. Beat together milk and pudding mix; add peel. Continue to beat a
few more seconds. Pour quickly over the top of the
mincemeat. Refrigerate at least 2 hours before serving.

BROWN SUGAR PUMPKIN PIE

1 1/2 Cups canned pumpkin
1 Cup packed brown sugar
1 Teaspoon cinnamon
1 Teaspoon nutmeg
1/2 Teaspoon allspice
3 Eggs, beaten
1 Cup evaporated milk
1 Unbaked 9" pie shell

Combine pumpkin, brown sugar, cinnamon, nutmeg and allspice. Add eggs and mix well. Gradually add evaporated milk, blend thoroughly. Pour into pie shell.Bake at 425 degrees for 15 minutes. Reduce heat to 350 degrees and bake additional 35-45 minutes or until knife inserted in middle comes out clean. Cool on wire rack.

ORANGE-SWEET POTATOES

3 Cups cooked mashed sweet potatoes
1 Cup brown sugar
3 Eggs, separated and beaten
1 Stick butter, melted
Juice and grated rind of one orange
1 Cup chopped English walnuts
1 Cup miniature marshmallows
1 Small can evaporated milk

Combine potatoes, sugar, egg yolks, butter, orange juice, milk and rind; beat well. Add walnuts and marsh-mallows. Beat egg whites until stiff but not dry; fold into mixture. Pour into greased casserole dish and bake at 350 degrees for 35 minutes.

LEMON CHESS PIE

2 Cups sugar
1 Tablespoon cornmeal
1 Tablespoon flour
4 Eggs
1/4 Cup milk
1/4 Cup lemon juice
1/4 Cup melted margarine
1/4 Teaspoon salt

Mix sugar, cornmeal and flour. Add eggs one at a time, beating after each addition. Pour in milk, lemon juice, melted margarine, and salt, mixing well. Pour into unbaked 9" pie shell and bake at 350 degrees for 1 hour 20 minutes - 1 1/2 hours.

OLD TIMEY BAKED CUSTARD

3 Eggs, beaten
1/4 Cup sugar
1/4 Teaspoon salt
2 Cups milk
1 Teaspoon vanilla
Nutmeg

Stir together eggs, sugar and salt. Slowly stir in milk and vanilla. Pour into custard cups and sprinkle with nutmeg. Bake in pan of water at 325 degrees 30-45 minutes or until knife inserted in middle comes out clean.

LUSCIOUS LEMON DESSERT

Crust:
2 Cups crushed fine vanilla wafers
1/2 Cup margarine, melted

Pour margarine over cookie crumbs and mix well.
Press into bottom of a casserole dish. Bake at 400
degrees for 10 minutes.

First layer:
3 3oz. Packages cream cheese, softened
1 Stick margarine, softened
2 Cups powdered sugar

Cream ingredients together until fluffy. Spread over
cookie crumbs.

Second layer:
2 Cans lemon pie filling or your choice of canned pie
filling
1 9oz. Container whipped topping.

Spread pie filling over cream cheese mixture. Top with
whipped topping. Garnish with fresh fruit to match the
filling. Completely chill before serving. Coconut is also
good toasted and sprinkled on top.

FRESH PEACH COBBLER

Make ahead pastry for 2 crust pies:

1 1/2 Cups sifted flour
1/2 Teaspoon salt
1/2 Cup shortening
4-5 Tablespoons ice water

Sift together flour and salt. Cut in shortening with pastry blender until pea-sized pellets form. Sprinkle water in a tablespoon at a time, mixing with fork. With hands, form a ball and set aside for a few minutes. Lightly flour pastry board, divide dough and roll into a ball. Place first ball on pastry board and flatten. Roll out and place into baking dish. Turn other half onto board and repeat procedure but making slightly larger than first. Fold second half into quarters, wrap in wax paper and place pastry in refrigerator until ready for use.

Filling:
1 Quart fresh sliced peaches
1 Cup sugar
1 Teaspoon vanilla
1 Tablespoon flour
3 Tablespoons water
1 Stick butter

Place peaches into a bowl, pour sugar over and stir. Stir flour into water. Stir until lumps are dissolved. Add vanilla. Pour into peaches and stir. Pour into prepared pastry and dot with butter until all is used. Unfold pastry and place on top of peaches, sealing at edges. With a knife, make slits (5) in center of pastry. Bake on a cookie sheet for 50-55 minutes or until crust is a deep golden brown.

PIE IN A POKE

1 9" Pie Crust
4 Large Granny Smith Apples
1 Cup brown sugar (more or less to taste)
1 Teaspoon lemon juice
2 Tablespoons flour
2 Teaspoons cinnamon

Rinse, peel and slice apples. Combine ingredients. Mix thoroughly. Pour into unbaked pie shell. Cover with topping.

Topping:
1 Stick margarine
1 Cup brown sugar
1 Cup flour

Melt margarine. Stir ingredients together. Spread dough over top of filling (dough will be sticky). Place in large paper bag and bake at 375 degree for 1 hour to 1 hour 15 minutes. Cool completely, in bag, before serving for a crunchy crust.

PECAN PIE

1 Cup light brown sugar
1/2 Cup white corn syrup
1/4 Cup melted butter
3 Eggs, beaten
1 Unbaked 9" pie shell
1 Cup pecans

Mix ingredients together. Pour into shell and bake for 50-60 minutes in a 350-degree oven or until filling is set.

EGG CUSTARD PIE

4 Eggs slightly beaten
1/2 Cup sugar
1/2 Teaspoon salt
1 1/2 Cups milk
1 Tablespoon butter

Combine eggs, sugar and salt. Stir well. Add milk, vanilla and butter, mixing well. Pour into 2 unbaked pie shells and sprinkle with nutmeg. Bake at 450 degrees for 10 minutes. Reduce temperature to 325 degrees and continue baking for 25 minutes.

"There was nothing
quite like Mama's
fresh pecan pie!"

SWEET POTATO PIE

1 1/2 Cups mashed sweet
  potatoes
3 Tablespoons margarine
3 Large eggs, beaten
2 Cups milk

1 1/4 Cup sugar
1/2 Teaspoon cinnamon
1/2 Teaspoon nutmeg
1/2 Teaspoon salt

Mix sweet potatoes, margarine, eggs and milk. Combine dry ingredients. Stir slowly into liquid mixture, mixing well. Pour into two 8" unbaked pie shells. Bake at 350 degrees for 40-50 minutes or until center is set.

FRIED APPLE PIES

Filling:
1 Package dried apples
1 Teaspoon cinnamon
1 Cup brown sugar
Prepared to package directions

Pastry:
2 Cups flour
1/2 Teaspoon salt
2/3 Cup shortening
6-7 Tablespoons ice water

Combine flour and salt. Cut in shortening with a pastry blender until size of small peas. Add water a tablespoon at a time and work with hands. Pinch off enough dough for each pie and place onto a floured pastry board and roll out thin, making small circles (I use small saucers to cut around). Place 1 1/2-2 Tablespoon of filling in center of each circle. Fold over, tuck edges under and crimp with fork. Fry on both sides in hot oil until brown.

BANANA SPLIT PIE

Crust:
2 Cups graham cracker crumbs
2 Tablespoons sugar
1 Stick butter, softened

Combine ingredients and press into pan. Bake in 400-degree oven for 8-10 minutes. Cool.

First layer:
2 3oz. Packages cream cheese, softened
2 Cups powdered sugar
1 Stick margarine, softened

Cream ingredients until light and fluffy. Spread over cooled crust.

Second layer:
4 Bananas, sliced
1 Can crushed pineapple, drained
1 Large container whipped topping

Slice bananas over first layer. Spread drained pineapple over bananas. Cover with whipped topping. Garnish with whole strawberries with caps and pecan halves.

CREAM CHEESE PASTRY AND FILLING

Pastry:
2 Sticks butter, softened
2 3oz. Packages cream cheese
2 Cups flour

Beat butter and cream cheese until well blended. Add flour, a half cup at a time. Work with hands until dough is smooth. Shape into 1" balls. Using a small cup muffin tin; place a ball in each cup and press down in middle with thumb.

Filling:
1 Stick butter, softened
1 Cup sugar
1 Cup English walnuts, chopped
1 Cup dried cranberries
1 Teaspoon vanilla
1/8 Teaspoon salt
2 Eggs, separated

Cream butter, sugar, salt and vanilla until light. Blend in beaten yolks. Stir in nuts and cranberries. Beat egg whites until stiff; fold into mixtures. Fill pastry cups and bake at 350 degrees for 15-20 minutes.

SWEET POTATO BALLS

1 1/2 Cups mashed sweet potatoes
1 Egg beaten
2 Tablespoons butter
1/4 Teaspoon cinnamon
Pinch of salt
1/2 Cup chopped raisins
1/2 Cup finely chopped pecans

Combine ingredients, except pecans, in order; mix well. Chill 30 minutes. Roll into small balls. Roll in nuts. Place on greased pan and bake at 375 degrees for 10-15 minutes depending on size of balls.

This is from our grandmother's time. In all truthfulness, we have never tried to make this recipe. We thought it would be intriguing to include it, in exact form, grammar, and spelling used. This is truly a look back into the American kitchen, from years gone by.

A VERY RICH AND DELICIOUS PLUM PUDDING

Chop finely 1/2 pound of suet, rub into it a small cupful of flour. Mix with it 3/4 of a pound of seeded raisins cut in two with the kitchen-scissors. Wash and dry 3/4 of a pound of currants and add. Take 1 3/4 cupfuls of sugar, 3 cupfuls of dried bread crumbs, 1/4 pound of sliced citron, 2 sour apples, peeled, cored and chopped fine. Mix all these thoroughly and then add a salt spoonful of salt and a half teaspoon of ground cloves, add also 6 well beaten eggs and moisten the whole with half a cupful of grape juice. This will make 2 puddings. Steam for 4 hours in 2 buttered* molds.

Sauce for plum pudding:
Mix one teaspoonful of corn starch with 1/2 cupful of sugar, add one cupful grape-juice and boil all together for 5 minutes, add 2 teaspoonfuls butter and serve hot.

* We couldn't quite make the writing out, but we believe it is "buttered."

BUTTERSCOTCH DELIGHT

Crust:
2/3 Cups margarine
1 1/2 Cups flour
1/2 Cup chopped pecans

Mix ingredients together. Press in bottom of a 9x13x2 pan. Bake at 375 degrees 15 minutes.

Layers:
1 8oz. Package cream cheese
1 Cup 10X sugar
1 Small container whipped topping, divided
2 Small boxes instant butterscotch pudding
3 Cups milk

Bring cheese to room temperature. Cream together with sugar. Add whipped topping and beat until smooth. Spread over cooled crust. Mix milk and pudding until lumps have dissolved. Spread over whipped mixture. Refrigerate for 1/2 hour. Spread additional whipped topping on top of chilled layers. Sprinkle nuts over top. You may use any flavor of pudding.

CHERRY YUM YUM

1 8oz. Package cream cheese
3/4 Cup 4X sugar
2 Envelopes whipped topping
1 Teaspoon vanilla
1 No.2 Can cherry pie filling
Graham cracker crust

Cream the cream cheese and sugar, add vanilla. Prepare whipped topping according to package directions. Add to creamed cheese mixture. Spread half of mixture over crust. Top with pie filling. Spread other half of mixture over top of pie filling. Chill several hours before serving.

CHERRIES IN THE SNOW

1 Box whipped topping
1 8oz. Package cream cheese
1 Cup powdered sugar
1 Angel food cake

Mix whipped topping according to package directions. Cream the cheese and powdered sugar until well blended. Layer a 9x13 casserole dish with whipped topping. Slice cake and place on topping. Make two layers finishing with topping. Spread cherry pie filling over top.

"To all things there is a season."

SOUTHERN LADIES
KNOW HOW TO COOK IT!

AMERICAN
TRADITIONS

"We always knew when Mama
was in the kitchen ...
the scent of homemade goodies
drifted all across the land."

CARROT CAKE

2 Cups sugar
4 Eggs
1 Teaspoon vanilla
1/2 cup oil
3/4 Cup buttermilk
2 Cups grated carrots
2 Cups flour
2 Teaspoon soda
1 Teaspoon baking powder
1/2 Teaspoon salt
1 1/2 Teaspoon cinnamon
1 8oz. Can crushed pineapple, drained
1 Cup chopped walnuts

Mix sugar, oil, vanilla, buttermilk and eggs until smooth. Sift together dry ingredients and stir into sugar mixture. Add carrots, pineapple and nuts, stirring just to mix. Pour into 2 greased and floured 9" layer pans. Bake at 350 degrees for 30-35 minutes. Cool 10 minutes before removing from pans. Cool completely before frosting.

Frosting:
1 8oz. Package cream cheese
1 Stick butter
1 1/2 Box powdered sugar
3/4 Teaspoon vanilla
1 Cup chopped walnuts

Combine ingredients except walnuts. Beat until light and fluffy. Fold in walnuts.

PEACH POUND CAKE

3/4 Cup vegetable oil
1 Cup sugar
3 Cups self-rising flour
5 Eggs
3 Teaspoons vanilla

3 Cups fresh peaches,
  peeled and chopped
1 Cup chopped nuts
1 Cup flaked coconut

Combine ingredients in order listed. Pour into greased, floured tube pan. Bake 1 hour or until done at 350 degrees. Cool 10 minutes before turning out onto wire rack. Cool completely before icing.

Peach Icing:
1 Medium peach, pureed
1 3oz. Package cream cheese
3/4 Cup coconut
1 1/2 Cups 4X sugar

Chop peaches and cover with sugar to make juice. Beat cream cheese and sugar. Add puree and coconut.

BEST CHEESE CAKE

5 8oz. packages cream cheese
1 3/4 Cups sugar
3 Tablespoons flour
1 Teaspoon vanilla

5 Eggs
2 Egg yolks
1/4 Cup whipping cream
1 Graham cracker crust

Crust:
1 Box of Graham Cracker crumbs
1 Cup of margarine (not butter) or enough margarine
  to form a ball
3 Tablespoons sugar

Prepare crust and line bottom and sides of springform pan. Combine cheese, sugar, flour and vanilla. Beat on high just to blend. Beat in eggs and yolks one at a time. Beat in whipping cream until just mixed. Pour into crust and bake 10 minutes at 500 degrees. Reduce to 250 degrees and bake 1 hour. Cool on wire rack completely before removing side of pan. Refrigerate. If desired, top with canned pie filling.

APPLESAUCE CAKE

1/2 Cup butter
3/4 Teaspoon salt
1/2 Teaspoon cinnamon
1/2 Teaspoon cloves
1/2 Teaspoon allspice
1/8 Teaspoon nutmeg
2 Tablespoons cocoa
1 1/2 Cups sugar

2 Eggs, unbeaten
1 1/2 Teaspoons soda
2 Cups sifted flour
3/4 Cup chopped dates
3/4 Cup chopped
   raisins
1 1/2 Cups apple sauce
3/4 Cup chopped nuts

Blend together butter, salt, spices, and cocoa. Add sugar and cream well. Add eggs, beating after each addition. Add soda to flour and sift 3 times. Sprinkle 2 tablespoons of flour over fruit. Add remaining flour to creamed mixture, along with apple sauce, mixing after each addition until smooth. Fold in nuts and fruit. Pour into greased and floured 10x10x2 baking pan. Bake at 350 degrees for 50 minutes to 1 hour.

PRUNE CAKE

2 Eggs
1 Cup brown sugar
3 Tablespoons butter
1 Cup cooked chopped
   prunes
1 Cup prune water

1/2 Teaspoon salt
1 Teaspoon vanilla
1 Teaspoon soda
2 Cups flour
1 Cup chopped English
   walnuts

Beat eggs, add ingredients in order, beating after each addition. Bake in a greased and floured bundt pan at 350 degree for 50 minutes to 1 hour or until done. Both cakes are good with or without frosting.

BANANA CAKE

1 Package yellow cake mix
1 Small package vanilla pudding
4 Eggs, beaten
1 Cup sour cream
1/2 Cup oil
1 Large banana, mashed

Combine ingredients in large mixing bowl. Beat for 5 minutes on medium speed. Pour into greased and floured tube or bundt pan. Bake at 350 degrees for 1 hour. Cool on wire rack for 15 minutes before removing from pan.

EVER SO EASY CAKE

2 Cups flour
2 Cups sugar
2 Teaspoons soda
1 Cup oil
2 Eggs, beaten
2 Cups crushed pineapp
1 Cup flaked coconut
1 Cup chopped nuts

Mix ingredients together well. Pour into a greased 9x13 baking pan. Bake at 350 degrees for 55 minutes to 1 hour. Pour icing over while hot.

Icing:
1 Cup sugar
1 Stick butter
1 Small can evaporated milk
1 Teaspoon vanilla
1 Cup flaked coconut

Bring sugar, butter and milk to a boil. Cook until sugar has dissolved (a couple of minutes). Remove from heat and add vanilla and coconut. Pour over cake.

HUMMINGBIRD CAKE

3 Cups flour
2 Cups sugar
1 Teaspoon salt
1 Teaspoon soda
1 Teaspoon cinnamon
3 Eggs, beaten
3/4 Cup oil
2 Teaspoons vanilla
2 Cups chopped bananas
1 Small can crushed pineapple, do not drain
1 Cup chopped walnuts

Combine dry ingredients in a large bowl. Add eggs and oil, stirring until moist. Don't beat. Stir in vanilla, bananas, pineapple and nuts. Stir until just mixed. Pour into three 8" greased and floured cake pans. Bake at 350 degrees for 25-30 minutes. Cool for 10 minutes before removing from pans.

Frosting:
1 8oz. Package cream cheese
3/4 Stick butter
2 Teaspoons vanilla
1 Box 10X Sugar

Combine ingredients. Mix on high until light and fluffy. If desired, fold in 1 cup walnuts

EASY RUM CAKE

1 Box yellow cake mix
1 Small package vanilla instant pudding
4 Eggs
1/2 Cup oil
1/2 Cup dark rum
1/2 Water
1 Cup pecan halves

Combine all ingredients except pecans. Mix well but don't overbeat. Grease and flour a tube pan and line with the pecan halves. Slowly pour mixture over. Bake in a 350-degree oven for 30-40 minutes or until done. Cool on wire rack for 10 minutes before removing from pan. Turn onto serving plate and pour glaze over while still warm.

Glaze:
1 Stick butter
1 Cup sugar
1/4 Cup water
1/2 Cup dark rum

Combine ingredients in a heavy saucepan. Boil for 5 minutes stirring constantly. Pour over cake using caution, extremely hot.

CHOCOLATE CARAMEL CAKE

1 Stick margarine
1 Cup sugar
4 Eggs, slightly beaten
1/2 Teaspoon vanilla
1 Cup self-rising flour
1/2 Teaspoon baking powder
1 Can chocolate syrup

Cream margarine, sugar and vanilla. Add rest of ingredients and mix for about 2 minutes. Pour into 8x10x2 prepared baking pan. Bake at 350 degrees, 35-40 minutes. Leave in pan. Pour topping over hot cake.

Topping:
1 Stick butter
1/2 Cup evaporated milk
1 Cup brown sugar

In a heavy sauce pan, combine ingredients and cook over medium heat for 2 1/2 minutes.

PRALINE BROWNIES

1 Cup sugar
1/2 Cup butter, softened
1/4 Cup butter
2 Eggs
1 Teaspoon vanilla
1/2 Cup light brown sugar
2 Tablespoons whipping cream
2 oz. Unsweetened chocolate, melted
3/4 Cup flour
3/4 Teaspoon salt
1 Cup chopped pecans, divided

Sift flour and salt and set aside. Cream together sugar and 1/2 cup of butter. Add eggs one at a time, beating after each addition. Mix in chocolate and vanilla. Add flour and salt. Fold in 1/2 cup of pecans. Pour into 8x8 baking pan that has been sprayed with non-stick spray. Bake at 400 degrees for 25-30 minutes.

While brownies are baking, cream together the 1/4 cup butter and brown sugar until light and fluffy. Whip in the cream. Fold in remaining pecans. Spread on top of hot brownies. Place back in oven under broiler until topping is bubbly.

BANANA NUT CAKE

1/2 Cup shortening
4 Medium bananas, mashed
3 Eggs
3 Cups plain flour
2 Cups sugar
1 1/2 Teaspoons baking powder
1 1/2 Teaspoons soda
1 Teaspoon salt
1 Teaspoon vanilla
1 Cup buttermilk
1 Cup walnuts

Cream shortening, bananas and eggs. Combine dry ingredients except walnuts and add to banana mixture, alternating with buttermilk that vanilla has been added to. Beat well but don't overbeat. Stir in walnuts. Pour into three 9" greased and floured layer pans. Bake at 350 degrees for 30-35 minutes. Cool completely before frosting.

Frosting:
1 Medium banana, mashed
1 Tablespoon fresh lemon juice
1 Box 4X sugar
1/2 Cup chopped walnuts

Whip bananas with lemon juice. Add sugar and continue to whip until spreading consistency. Fold in nuts. Frost cake.

Helpful hint: Wipe any lose crumbs off of cake layers and sprinkle powdered sugar on top of each when cooled. This will prevent the frosting from being absorbed into the layers.

SWEET POTATO CAKE

1/2 Cup oil
2 Cups sugar
4 Eggs, divided
1/4 Cup scalded milk
2 1/2 Cups sifted cake flour
3 Teaspoons baking powder
1 1/2 Teaspoons cinnamon
1/2 Teaspoon nutmeg
1 Teaspoon vanilla
1 1/2 Cups uncooked grated sweet potatoes
1 Cup each: frozen coconut and nuts

Sift together dry ingredients and set aside. Combine oil and sugar and beat until smooth. Add egg yolks, beating well. Pour milk into egg mixture and beat just until blended. Add dry ingredients and beat well. Stir in vanilla, sweet potatoes, coconut and nuts. Beat egg whites until stiff but not dry. Fold into batter. Bake in three 9" layer pans at 350 degrees for 30 minutes. Cool in pans on wire racks for 10 minutes before removing. Cool completely before frosting with coconut cream cheese frosting.

Frosting:
1 8oz. Package cream cheese
1 Stick margarine, softened
1 Teaspoon vanilla
1 1/2 Boxes174 powdered sugar
1/2 Cup frozen coconut

Cream together cheese and margarine. Beat in sugar and vanilla until light and fluffy. Frost cooled cake. Sprinkle coconut on top.

SISSY'S APPLE STACK CAKE

1/2 Cup shortening
1 Cup sugar
2 Eggs, well beaten
1/2 Cup molasses
1/2 Cup buttermilk
1 Teaspoon vanilla

1 Teaspoon baking powder
1 Teaspoon soda
1/4 Teaspoon salt
4 Cups flour
1 Teaspoon cinnamon

Cream shortening and sugar. Add eggs, molasses, buttermilk and vanilla. Combine dry ingredients, mixing thoroughly. Work into creamed mixture until you have a stiff dough. Roll out on floured pastry board until thin (about 1/4"). You will have five or six layers, depending on pan size. Bake at 350 degrees for 10-12 minutes. When cool, stack layers with highly spiced fruit in between each layer (we like dried apples). Wrap and store in refrigerator at least 2 days before serving.

PUMPKIN CAKE

2 Cups sugar
1 Cup shortening
3 Large eggs
1 Teaspoon vanilla
2 Cups flour
1 1/2 Teaspoons salt
2 Teaspoons soda
2 Teaspoons cinnamon
2 Cans canned pumpkin

Cream sugar and shortening. Add eggs, one at a time. Beat after each addition. Beat in vanilla. Combine dry ingredients and add to creamed mixture. Fold in pumpkin. Pour into prepared bundt pan and bake at 350 degrees for 1 hour. Good with or without frosting.

PINEAPPLE UPSIDE DOWN CAKE

Bottom:
1 Cup butter, melted
1 1/2 Cups brown sugar
9 Pineapple slices
9 Maraschino cherry halves

Batter:
1 Cup shortening
1 1/2 Cups sugar
3 Eggs, beaten
1 1/2 Cups cake flour
1 Tablespoon baking powder
1/2 Teaspoon salt
1 Cup milk
2 Teaspoons vanilla

Pour melted butter into an oblong baking pan. Stir in brown sugar. Place pineapple rings in rows on top of this. Insert cherry half in center of each pineapple ring, set aside.

Cream shortening and sugar together until light. Add eggs and vanilla, beat well. Combine dry ingredients and add to creamed mixture, alternating with milk until smooth. Pour over pineapple. Bake at 350 degrees for 35-40 minutes. Cool for 15 minutes before turning out. Use caution, very hot.

DUMP CAKE

1/2 Box yellow cake mix
1 Large can fruit pie filling
1 Stick margarine
1/2 Cup chopped nuts

In an 8"x8"x2" baking pan, pour dry cake mix on bottom and smooth out. Pour fruit filling (use your favorite) on top of cake mix and spread. Cut butter into small pats and lay on top of filling. Sprinkle with nuts. Bake 20-30 minutes in a 350-degree oven. To serve, dip out with spoon. Delicious!!

PISTACHIO CAKE

1 Package yellow cake mix
3/4 Cup oil
1 Small package instant
   pistachio pudding
3 Eggs, slightly beaten
3/4 Cup flaked coconut
1Cup chopped pecans
1 Cup citrus soda

Mix ingredients in order listed. Pour into 3 greased and floured 8" layer pans. Bake at 350 degrees 30-35 minutes or until done. Cool on wire racks for 10 minutes before turning out.

Frosting:
1 Large container whipped topping
1/2 Cup milk
1/2 Cup flaked coconut
1/2 Cup pistachio nuts
1 Small package instant pistachio pudding

Beat all ingredients except nuts until spreading consistency. Frost cooled cake. Garnish with coconut and nuts.

COCONUT CAKE

2 Sticks butter, softened
2 Cups sugar
3 Cups flour
4 Eggs
1 Cup milk
2 Teaspoons baking powder
2 Teaspoons vanilla

Sift flour and baking powder together and set aside.
Cream butter and sugar. Add eggs one at a time, beating
after each addition. Add flour and milk alternately. Stir
in vanilla and mix well. Pour into 4 well-greased and
floured layer pans, with an equal amount in each pan.
Bake at 350 degrees until center of cake springs back
when lightly touched.

Icing:
2 Egg whites, room temperature
1 1/2 Cups sugar
1/4 Cup + 1 tablespoon water
2 Tablespoons white corn syrup
Pinch of salt
2 Packages frozen coconut, thawed

Combine egg whites, sugar, water and corn syrup in
top of double boiler. Cook beating constantly for 7 minutes or until peaks form. Remove from heat and add the
salt and beat well. Spread icing between layers. Sprinkle
each layer with coconut. Ice top and sides cake and
sprinkle coconut on top and lightly pat on sides.

CHOCOLATE CAKE
WITH MELTAWAY ICING

2 Cups sugar
1 Stick butter, softened
1/2 Cup oil
2 Eggs
2 Cups flour
1/4 Cup cocoa
1 Teaspoon soda
1/2 Teaspoon salt
1 Teaspoon vanilla
1 Cup buttermilk
1/2 Cup water

Cream sugar, butter, and oil. Add eggs one at a time, beating after each addition. Combine dry ingredients; add to creamed mixture a little at a time, alternating with buttermilk. Beat in vanilla and half cup of water. Pour into greased oblong baking pan and bake at 325 degrees for 45 minutes or until center springs back when lightly touched. Five minutes before cake is done, prepare the icing.

Icing:
1 Stick butter
1/4 Cup cocoa
1/4 Cup+2 tablespoons whole milk
1 Box powdered sugar

Pour sugar into a mixing bowl and set aside. Melt butter in a small saucepan; add the milk and cocoa and bring to a full boil stirring constantly. Pour over sugar and beat well. Stick the tines of a fork into hot cake for icing to soak in. Pour icing over, cover entire surface.

LEMON NUT POUND CAKE

2/3 Cups butter
1 1/4 Cups sugar
1 Tablespoon lemon juice
2/3 Cup milk
1 Teaspoon salt
2 1/4 Cups flour
3/4 Chopped pecans
1 Teaspoon baking powder
3 Eggs

Cream butter and sugar until fluffy. Add lemon juice then milk, beating after each addition. Combine flour, salt and baking powder; add to shortening mixture. Mix at low speed for a couple of minutes. Add eggs 1 at a time, mixing between each addition. Stir in chopped nuts. Pour into greased and floured tube pan. Bake at 300 degrees for 1 hour 15-20 minutes. Cool on wire rack for 15 minutes before removing from pan.

PINEAPPLE CAKE
(EASY AND SIMPLE)

Layers:
1 Package yellow cake mix, bake according to directions on box

Frosting:
1 Large container whipped topping
1 Can crushed pineapple, drained
1 Cup sour cream

Stir together all frosting ingredients, mixing well. Frost cooled cake layers. Refrigerate.

KENTUCKY POUND CAKE

4 Eggs, separated
2 Cups sugar
1/2 Cup oil
1 Teaspoon vanilla
2 1/2 Cups self-rising flour
1 Cup crushed pineapple, drained
2 Tablespoons hot water
2 Teaspoons cinnamon
1 Cup chopped walnuts

Stir together egg yolks, sugar, oil and vanilla. Add
flour, pineapple, water and cinnamon, beating as you go.
Set aside. Beat egg whites until stiff. Gently stir nuts
into whites. Fold into the batter. Pour into a greased
and floured tube pan. Bake at 350 degrees for 1 hour
and 10 minutes. Cool in pan on wire rack 10-15 minutes
before removing.

BANANA NUT POUND CAKE

1 Cup oil
2 Cups sugar
1 Teaspoon vanilla
3 Eggs, well beaten
3 Cups flour
1 Teaspoon soda
1/2 Teaspoon salt
1/2 Cup buttermilk
1 1/2 Cups mashed
   bananas
1 Cup chopped pecans

Stir together oil, sugar and vanilla. Add eggs. With a
mixer, beat buttermilk and bananas. Sift together flour,
soda and salt. Combine all ingredients except pecans.
Mix well but don't overbeat. Fold in pecans. Pour into
prepared bundt pan. Bake at 325 degrees for 1 hour 20
minutes.

ICE BOX FRUIT CAKE

1 Box graham crackers
1 Bag small marshmallows
1 Large can evaporated milk
1 Package frozen coconut
1 Box light raisins
1 Large jar maraschino cherries
1 1/2 Pounds shelled pecans

Crush graham crackers in a large bowl and set aside.
Combine canned milk and half the bag of marshmallows
in a heavy sauce pan. Cook on low, stirring constantly,
until marshmallows have dissolved. Pour over cracker
crumbs. Add rest of marshmallows and other ingredients
and mix well (I use my hands). Pour into airtight oblong
container and press flat. Refrigerate 2-3 days before
serving. If serving a large crowd, double the recipe.

COCONUT POUND CAKE

3 Sticks butter
3 Cups sugar
6 Large eggs
3 Cups flour
1 Can flaked coconut

1 Teaspoon baking
    powder
1/4 Teaspoon salt
1 Teaspoon vanilla
1 Can evaporated milk

Cream butter and sugar. Add eggs one at a time. Beat
after each addition. Sift together dry ingredients. Stir
vanilla into milk. Add dry ingredients alternately with
milk, beating as you go. Stir in coconut. Pour into prepared bundt pan and bake at 350 degrees for 1 hour and
15 minutes. Cool in pan for 10 minutes before removing.

SPICE CAKE WITH BAKED FROSTING

1/4 Cup shortening
3/4 Cup brown sugar
1 Egg, beaten
1 3/8 Cups cake flour
1 Teaspoon baking powder
1/4 Teaspoon soda
1/2 Teaspoon cinnamon
1/4 Teaspoon cloves
1/4 Teaspoon salt
1/4 Cup chopped dates
1/2 Cup sour milk

Cream shortening and sugar. Beat in egg. Sift dry ingredients together. Combine with creamed mixture alternately with sour milk. Fold in chopped dates. Pour into greased 8"x8"x2" pan and bake at 375 degrees for 30-35 minutes.

Baked Frosting:
2 Egg whites
1/4 Teaspoon salt
1 Cup brown sugar
1/4 Teaspoon vanilla
1/4 Cup chopped nuts

Beat egg whites until firm. Gradually add sugar. To this add salt, vanilla and nuts. Spread on the batter and sprinkle with additional nuts. Bake as specified above.

RED VELVET CAKE

1 1/2 Cups sugar
1 Cup shortening
2 Large eggs
2 Tablespoons cocoa
2 2oz. Bottle red food color
2 1/4 Cups flour
1 Teaspoon salt
1 Cup buttermilk
1 Tablespoon vinegar
1 Teaspoon soda

Cream sugar and shortening and add eggs, one at time.
Make a paste with food coloring and cocoa; add to shortening mixture. Combine flour and salt and add. Mix
buttermilk, vinegar and soda in a cup; add to batter.
Pour into 3 greased and floured 8" layer pans. Bake at
350 degrees for 25-30 minutes or until done. Cool in
pans for 10 minutes before removing.

Frosting:
1 Box 4X Sugar
1/2 Teaspoon vanilla
1 8oz. Package cream cheese
1/2 Cup chopped pecans
4 Tablespoons margarine

Bring cheese and margarine to room temperature.
Cream together all ingredients until light and fluffy. If
too thin, add more 4Xsugar.

BUTTERMILK PRUNE CAKE

1 1/2 Cups sugar
1Cup shortening
2 Large eggs
1 Cup buttermilk
1 Teaspoon soda
2 Teaspoons vanilla
2 Cups flour
1 Teaspoon cinnamon
1/2 Teaspoon nutmeg
2 Cups cooked prunes, chopped
1 1/2 Cups walnuts pieces

Cream shortening and sugar. Add eggs. Stir soda and vanilla into buttermilk. Add dry ingredients, except prunes and nuts, alternating with buttermilk, beating after each addition. Fold in prunes and nuts. Pour into greased and floured bundt pan and bake in a 300-degree oven for 1 hour or until done. Cool on wire racks for 10 minutes before removing from pans. Cool completely before frosting.

CREAM CHEESE FROSTING

2 8oz. Packages cream cheese
2 Boxes powdered sugar
1 Stick margarine
2 Teaspoons vanilla

Beat cream cheese and margarine together. Add sugar, beat well. Add vanilla and continue beating until of spreading consistency. This makes a lot of frosting. I usually make this when I'm baking a couple of cakes. For a smaller amount, cut recipe in half.

LADY BALTIMORE CAKE

2 Cups flour
1 Cup butter (no substitute)
2 Cups sugar
1 Cup whole milk
2 Teaspoons baking powder
4 Eggs, divided
1 Teaspoon vanilla extract
1 Teaspoon lemon extract

Sift together flour and baking powder and set aside. Cream butter and sugar; add egg yolks, one at a time, beating well after each addition. Add milk and then flour, baking powder and extracts, mixing well. Beat egg whites until stiff; fold into batter. Pour into three 9" greased and floured layer pans. Bake at 350 degrees for 30 minutes or until center of cake springs back when lightly touched.

Filling:

2 Cups sugar
1 Fresh medium lemon
Water
2 Cups fresh coconut
3/4 Cup pecans, chopped
1/2 Cup light raisins

1 Small jar maraschino cherries, chopped
3/4 Cup crushed pineapple, drained
2 Teaspoons flour
2 Tablespoons cold wat

Squeeze juice of lemon into a measuring cup, adding enough water to bring up to one cup. In a heavy saucepan, combine water and sugar. Heat until it comes to a rolling boil. Add coconut, pecans, raisins, cherries and pineapple. Continue to cook on medium heat for 10 minutes. While filling is cooking, stir flour into cold water and beat until lumps are dissolved. Just before removing filling from heat, stir flour mixture in to thicken. When cake layers and filling have cooled, spread filling between layers.

CHERRY POUND CAKE

1 Cup shortening
1 Stick butter
3 Cups sugar
6 Eggs
3 3/4 Cups cake flour
Large jar Maraschino cherries
2 tsp. Butternut flavoring
3/4 Cup milk

Chop cherries and set aside. Cream shortening, butter and sugar together. Add eggs one at a time and beat well. Add flour alternately with milk. Add vanilla and fold in cherries. Bake in a cold oven for 2 hours. (325° - do not preheat)

BUTTERNUT FROSTING

2 Pounds powdered sugar
1 Cup shortening
1/2 Cup milk
1 Teaspoon salt
1 Teaspoon butternut flavor

Mix ingredients and beat for 10- 15 minutes. This will keep in refrigerator for a couple of months if covered tightly. Use as needed. May use vanilla instead of butternut, if desired.

APPLE CAKE

1 Cup shortening
3 Eggs
2 Cups brown sugar
1 1/2 Teaspoons vanilla
2 Cups flour
1 Teaspoon salt
1 Teaspoon cinnamon
1 Teaspoon baking soda
1 Cup chopped walnuts
3 Cups Granny Smith apples, sliced

Cream shortening, eggs, sugar and vanilla. Combine flour, salt, cinnamon and soda. Add to shortening mixture; beat well but don't overbeat. Fold in apples and nuts. Pour into greased and floured oblong baking pan. Bake at 300 degrees for 1 hour or until done. Cool completely before frosting.

Frosting:
1 Stick margarine, softened
1 Cup brown sugar
1 Teaspoon vanilla
1/4 Cup evaporated milk
10X Sugar

Combine margarine and brown sugar in a heavy sauce pan, stirring constantly to avoid scorching. Add evaporated milk and vanilla. Cook until smooth. Use as much 10X sugar as needed while beating to bring the frosting to spreading consistency.

MERINGUE CAKE WITH RASPBERRIES

4 Tablespoons shortening
1 Cup sugar
2 Eggs, separated
1 Cup flour
2 Teaspoons baking powder
1/4 Teaspoon salt
7 Tablespoons milk
1/2 Teaspoon vanilla

Cream shortening and gradually add 1/2 cup of sugar, creaming well. Add egg yolks, one at a time, while beating. Sift together flour, baking powder and salt. Add to mixture. Combine milk and vanilla and beat into batter. Pour into greased square baking pan (8x8x2). Beat egg whites until foamy. Add remaining sugar, 2 tablespoons at a time, while beating, until mixture peaks. Pile on batter and bake at 350 degrees for 50 minutes. Remove and let stand 10 minutes, then loosen edges. Cut into squares and top with crushed raspberries.

POUND CAKE

1/2 Cup shortening
2 Sticks butter
1 1/2 Teaspoons vanilla
5 Large eggs
3 Cups sifted cake flour
1/2 Teaspoon baking powder
3 Cups sugar
1 Cup milk

Cream shortening, butter and sugar. Add eggs one at a time, beating after each addition. Add flour, baking powder, and milk alternately; stir in vanilla. Pour into greased and floured tube pan. Bake at 325 degrees for 1 1/2 hours. Cool in pan on wire rack for 15 minutes before removing.

COCONUT CAKE

1 Package yellow cake mix
1 Cup milk
1 Cup sugar
1 Large container whipped topping
2 Packages frozen coconut

Prepare cake according to package directions and bake in an oblong baking pan. Remove from oven and cool on a wire rack. While cooling, poke holes all over cake (about an inch apart) with the end of a wooden spoon. Heat milk and sugar over medium heat until sugar has dissolved. Pour over warm cake. Cover loosely and refrigerate. When cake is cold, cover with the whipped topping. Sprinkle thawed coconut over topping. Cover and refrigerate.

LEMON CAKE

1 Small package lemon gelatin
1 Cup hot water
1 Package lemon cake mix
3/4 Cup oil
4 Eggs

Dissolve gelatin in boiling water and cool. Combine cake mix, oil and eggs. Mix thoroughly. Add the gelatin and beat until smooth. Pour into a greased and floured oblong pan and bake at 350 degrees for 30 minutes or until nicely brown. Pour glaze over immediately.

Glaze:
Mix juice of 3 lemons and 2 cups confectioners sugar. Grate rind of 1 lemon and add to juice and sugar mixture. Pour over cake.

APPLE CRISP

4 Cups sliced Granny Smith apples
1 Teaspoon lemon juice
3/4 Cup brown sugar
1/2 Teaspoon cinnamon

Combine ingredients and place in greased baking dish.

Topping:
1/2 Cup oatmeal
3/4 Teaspoon cinnamon
1/4 Cup flour
4 Tablespoons butter
1/2 Cup brown sugar

Combine dry ingredients. Cut in butter until coarsely textured. Sprinkle over the apple mixture. Bake at 350 degrees 30-35 minutes or until nicely browned. Serve topped with vanilla ice cream.

QUICK LEMON PIE

1 Can sweetened condensed milk
Juice of 3 lemons
1 Teaspoon grated lemon rind
1- 9oz. Carton whipped topping
1 Graham cracker crust

Combine milk, lemon juice and whipped topping, mixing thoroughly. Sprinkle rind over mixture and fold in. Pour into pie crust. Garnish with lemon rind curls and chill.

YAM PIE

2 Cups oatmeal
1 1/2 Cups self-rising flour
1 Cup butter or margarine
1 Cup brown sugar
1 Teaspoon vanilla
1 16 oz can yams, mashed
1 Can sweetened condensed milk
2 Eggs, beaten
1 1/2 Teaspoons allspice
1/2 Cup chopped nuts

Combine oatmeal and flour, set aside. Beat margarine, sugar and vanilla until fluffy. Add dry ingredients, mix until crumbly. Save 3/4 cup of crumb mixture for later. Press rest of mixture into a 13x9x2 baking pan. Bake 10-12 minutes at 350 degrees. Combine remaining ingredients (except nuts and reserved mixture), mixing well. Pour mixture over crust. Combine reserved crumbs and nuts. Sprinkle evenly over top. Bake at 350 degrees for 25-30 minutes or until brown.

BEVERAGE

"Memories live
forever and thats
a fact. To recall
something precious,
one just has
to think back."

SOUTHERN LADIES
KNOW HOW TO COOK IT!

MEMORIES

COOKIN' UP MEMORIES

As we walk down roads we haven't visited in some
time,
My mind goes back to a world filled with sunshine.
To a summer of climbing over vine-covered hills.
Of blackberry picking you, me, Sandy and Bill.
We visited old Curly on the way to the barn,
Passing the summer, never doing no harm.
Looking forward to Sissy's blackberry pies.
Oh, how we miss our family ties.
But I have you, and you have me,
And we can always cook up old memories.

Rosemary Arrington Newman

CRANBERRY PUNCH

1 64oz. Bottle cranberry juice, chilled
1 2 Liter bottle ginger ale, chilled
1 Large can frozen orange juice, thawed

Combine ingredients in large punch bowl. Float a pretty iced fruit ring in punch just before serving.

MAMA'S SPECIAL OCCASION PUNCH

1 Large can pineapple juice, chilled
1 2-Liter bottle ginger ale, chilled
1/2 Gallon lime sherbet, softened.

In a large punch bowl, stir ingredients together just before time to serve.

This was our mother's favorite punch for special occasions, such as baby showers, bridal showers and weddings. She would change the flavor of sherbet to suit the occasion.

CRANBERRY CHRISTMAS PUNCH

1 Small box cherry gelatin
1 Cup boiling water
1 6oz. Can frozen lemonade
3 Cups cold water
1 Quart cranberry juice cocktail
1 2-Liter bottle ginger ale

Dissolve gelatin in boiling water. Stir in frozen lemonade concentrate. In large punch bowl, add cold water
and cranberry juice. Stir in gelatin mixture. When ready
to serve, pour in chilled ginger ale. Float a molded ice
ring.

QUICK PUNCH

2 Packages lime-flavored drink mix
1 Cup sugar
2 Large cans pineapple juice
12-Liter bottle ginger ale

Combine drink mix, sugar and pineapple juice in a
large punch bowl. Stir until sugar has dissolved. Pour in
chilled ginger ale. Serve over crushed ice.

RUSSIAN TEA

1 7oz. jar orange breakfast drink
1/2 Cup instant tea with lemon
1/2 Teaspoon ground cloves
1 Cup sugar
3/4 Teaspoon cinnamon

Mix ingredients in a container that can be covered tightly. Bring 1 cup water to a low boil. Stir in 1-2 teaspoons of mixture until dissolved. Cover and store rest of mixture until needed.

POWDERED CHOCOLATE MILK

10 Cups dry powdered milk
1-Pound can instant chocolate mix
2 Cups 4X sugar
16oz. Jar coffee creamer

Mix ingredients. Bring water to boil for as many cups as needed. Stir in 1/4 cup dry mixture until dissolved. Store unused mixture in airtight container

Our sister, Phoebe, gives this to us in a beautifully decorated jar along with mugs at Christmas. It's a gift we always look forward to and it lasts well into the winter.

OLD FASHIONED CHOCOLATE

1 oz. Unsweetened chocolate
1 Tablespoon sugar
2 Tablespoons hot water
2 Cups scalded milk
1/2 Teaspoon vanilla

Cut chocolate into small pieces. In a heavy saucepan, add chocolate, sugar and hot water. Cook until smooth. Gradually add scalded milk, stirring constantly. Reduce heat and simmer additional 5 minutes.

COCOA FOR TWO

1 1/3 Tablespoons cocoa
1 1/3 Tablespoons sugar
2 Tablespoons cold water
1 1/2 Cup milk

Mix cocoa with sugar and cold water. Cook over medium low heat until thick. Add milk and stir. Boil for 1 minute. You may use more sugar, if desired. Garnish with miniature marshmallows or whipped cream.

WINE PUNCH

1/2 Gallon red wine
1 6oz. Can lime concentrate
1 6oz. Can lemonade
3 oz. Lemon juice
1 Quart lemon lime soda

Combine wine and juices in punch bowl. Float colorful ice ring. Pour soda over. Garnish with lemon and lime slices.

AFTER THOUGHTS

ᴄ SOUTHERN LADIES ᴄ
KNOW HOW TO COOK IT!

COOKIN' UP
FUN!

CORNBREAD STUFFING

4 Cups cornbread
3 Tablespoons onion
1 Teaspoon salt
1/4 Teaspoon black pepper
Chopped giblets
1/4 Teaspoon poultry seasoning
1 Cup chopped celery
Sage to taste
1/3 Cup margarine, melted
Broth to moisten

Combine dry ingredients. Melt margarine in broth. Pour over dry ingredients until moist. Spoon into baking pan and smooth to sides. Bake at 375 degrees for about 35 minutes. Use enough broth or stuffing will be dry.

MARINADE

1 1/2 Cup salad oil
3/4 Cup soy sauce
1/3 Cup fresh lemon juice
4 Tablespoons Worcestershire sauce
2 Tablespoons dry mustard
2 Teaspoons salt
1 Teaspoon black pepper
1/2 Cup wine vinegar
1 1/2 Teaspoon parsley flakes
2 Garlic cloves, crushed

Combine ingredients, mix well. Place meat in marinade for several hours. If meat isn't covered, turn halfway through. The longer the meat is left in sauce, the more flavorful and tender it will be. Discard sauce once meat is removed. Never baste meat with leftover sauce. This sauce is great for beef or chicken.

APPLESAUCE

4 Cups sliced Granny Smith apples
Cold water
3/4 Cup sugar
1/2 Teaspoon lemon rind

Place sliced apples in a large, heavy saucepan. Add water to almost cover. Cook slowly until soft. Add sugar, stirring well and continue to cook for a few more minutes. Remove from heat. Stir in lemon rind. Good hot or cold. You may vary recipe by adding brown sugar instead of white, and cinnamon instead of sugar.

BROWN SAUCE

1 Tablespoon butter
1 Tablespoon flour
1 Cup beef stock
Salt and pepper

Brown butter in saucepan. Add flour, stirring constantly until brown and smooth. Pour in stock and stir until thickened. Simmer 4 or 5 minutes. Excellent on rice or mashed potatoes.

STRAWBERRY PIZZA

Crust: 1 1/2 Cups flour
1 1/2 Sticks margarine, melted
3/4 Cups chopped pecans
1 Tablespoon sugar
1/8 Teaspoon salt

Mix ingredients well. Press into a pizza pan. Bake at 350 degrees for 10 minutes.

Filling:
1 8oz. Package cream cheese
2 Cups powdered sugar
2 Cups whipped topping

Cream the cheese and sugar together until fluffy. Fold in the whipped topping. Spread on cooled crust. Place 2 cups sliced strawberries on top of filling.

Topping:
2 Cups chopped strawberries
3/4 Cup sugar
2 Tablespoons cornstarch
1/3 Cup cold water

Stir flour into water until all lumps are dissolved. Combine ingredients and cook on medium heat until thick. Cool and stir in a few drops of red food coloring. Spread on top of strawberries and chill.

BULLS EYE EGGS

6 Slices bread
6 Eggs
Grease for frying

Cut a 2" hole in center of each slice of bread. Place in hot grease in frying pan. Quickly break an egg into each hole. Cook on both sides. Season and serve.

BACON WITH SWEET POTATO PUFFS

1 Pound bacon, fried
6 Slices pineapple
3 Cups mashed sweet potatoes
1/2 Cup milk
Plenty of butter (to taste)
6 Large marshmallows

Combine sweet potatoes, milk and butter. Whip until very fluffy; pile on pineapple rings and top with marshmallows. Bake in a 375-degree oven for about 20 minutes or until marshmallows are brown and pineapple slices are hot. Serve while hot, along with fried bacon.

CHEESE GRITS

4 Cups boiling water
1 Cup grits
Salt to taste
1 Tablespoon Worcestershire sauce (optional)
1 Stick margarine
1/2 Pound sharp Cheddar cheese, grated

Cook grits in boiling water until completely done and thickened. Add Worcestershire sauce, margarine and cheese. Stir until margarine and cheese have melted. Serve hot. Excellent with fish. Can also be placed, when cooked and mixed, in greased casserole dish and baked at 350 degrees for 20 minutes. Either way is delicious!

SHRIMP AND FRIED GRITS

2 Cups cold cooked grits
1 Tablespoon bacon drippings
2 Pounds shrimp, cooked and peeled
1 Cup Half and Half
1 Tablespoon cornstarch
1/4 Cup seafood seasoning
1/4 Cup white wine

A couple of hours before preparing dish, cook grits following package directions. Pour into shallow pan and allow to cool. Cut into wedges. Place in hot bacon drippings and fry, browning on both sides.. While grits are frying, combine rest of ingredients, except shrimp. heat in saucepan until thickened, simmering 2 or 3 minutes. Add shrimp to sauce and simmer 2 minutes more. Arrange grit wedges on platter and pour sauce over.

LEMON CHEESE SALAD

1 Package lemon gelatin
1 Cup boiling water
2 Cups Cottage cheese
3 Tablespoons mayonnaise
1 Small can evaporated milk
1/2 Cup shredded coconut
1/2 Cup chopped pecans
1/4 Cup maraschino cherries

Dissolve gelatin in boiling water. Combine rest of ingredients and stir into gelatin. Chill until firm

LIME PINEAPPLE SALAD

1 Package lime gelatin
3 Cups pineapple juice
1 Can sweetened condensed milk
1 Teaspoon creamed horseradish
2 Cups miniature marshmallows
1 Small carton cottage cheese
1/2 Cup maraschino cherries

Boil pineapple juice. Remove from heat and stir in gelatin. Allow to cool. Stir in pineapple. Mix together rest of ingredients and stir into gelatin mixture. Refrigerate until firm.

Both of the above make beautiful molded salads.

CHICKEN AND CORN CHOWDER

2-3 Pounds fryer parts
Water to cover
1 Teaspoon salt
1/4 Teaspoon black pepper
2 1/2 Cups cream style corn
Chopped parsley

Rinse chicken parts and place in a large pot. Cover with water and add salt; bring to a boil. Reduce heat and cook until tender. Remove chicken from broth and allow to cool. Remove meat from bones and return chicken to pot. Heat and add black pepper and corn. Simmer for 15 minutes. Pour into bowls and garnish with parsley.

CHICKEN RICE SOUP

2-3 Pounds chicken parts
6 Cups water
1/2 Cup chopped green onions, including blades
1/2 Cup diced celery
1/2 Cup diced carrots
2 Cups uncooked rice

Rinse chicken and place in large pot. Bring to boil, reduce heat and cook until tender. Remove chicken from broth and allow to cool. Add water to broth bring back up to 6 cups. While chicken is cooling, pour vegetables and rice into broth and cook on medium low until rice is tender. Remove chicken from bones and place chicken back in pot. Discard bones. Reduce heat and simmer for 15 minutes. Serve hot.

DEVILED EGGS

8-10 Hard boiled eggs
2 Heaping teaspoons sweet pickle cubes
2 Rounded tablespoons mayonnaise
Pinch of salt and pepper

Split eggs lengthwise. Remove yolks and place in bowl.
Be careful not to damage whites. Mash yolks with fork.
Combine yolks, pickles, mayonnaise, salt and pepper.
Mix well. Spoon mixture into whites. Garnish with
paprika. Cover and refrigerate until ready to use.

HAM AND VEGGIE OMELET

3 Large eggs
3 Tablespoons milk
Salt and pepper to taste
1/3 Cup chopped, cooked ham
3 Tablespoons chopped green pepper
3 Tablespoon chopped green onion

In a bowl, combine eggs, milk, salt and pepper. Beat with
a fork. Spray a large frying pan with non-stick spray and
heat. Pour egg mixture into pan. Scatter ham and vegetables on top of eggs on one side only. When eggs
become firm enough to turn, fold empty side over the
meat and vegetable side. Flip once and continue cooking
for a few more seconds. Remove from pan and garnish
with fresh tomato wedges. Enough for two people.

POTATO SOUP

3 Cups mashed potatoes
3 Cups milk
1 Small onion
1/2 Teaspoon salt
1/4 Teaspoon pepper
1 Tablespoon butter
3 or 4 slices bacon

Fry bacon. Drain on paper towels and set aside. Saute onion in bacon drippings until tender. In a heavy saucepan, combine milk, butter, salt and pepper, add onions. Heat on medium until almost boiling. Add potatoes, stirring well. Crumble bacon and add to soup. Simmer 10-15 minutes.

GERMAN POTATO SOUP

4 Large potatoes
2 large onions
3 Bay leaves
1 Quart milk
2 Egg yolks, beaten
Salt and pepper to taste
1 Tablespoon butter
Minced parsley

Boil potatoes, onions and bay leaves in salted water until done. Drain. Mash potatoes and onion. Add milk, egg yolks, salt and pepper. Add butter and simmer for a few minutes more. Remove bay leaves; spoon into individual serving bowls and sprinkle each with parsley. Serve with crisp wafers.

MATRIMONIAL BARS

1 Cup quick oatmeal
3/4 Cups brown sugar
1/2 Cup shortening
1 Cup flour
1/2 Teaspoon soda
1/2 Teaspoon salt
1/2 Cup buttermilk

Cream shortening and sugar. Sift flour, soda and salt. Add oatmeal. Add to creamed mixture alternately with buttermilk. Roll out on floured pastry board. Place half the dough into greased shallow pan. Spread on filling and top with remaining dough. Bake in a 350-degree oven for 25-30 minutes. Cut into bars when partially cool.

Filling:
1/2 pound stewed prunes
1/2 Cup water
1/4 Cup brown sugar
Juice and rind of small orange

Combine all ingredients and bring to a boil. Cook until thickened. Spread on first half of dough.

OLD TIMEY TOMATOES AND RICE

1 Cup rice
1 Large onion
2 Cups milk
1 Can tomatoes
2 Tablespoons butter
Salt and pepper to taste

Bring milk to boil over medium heat. Pour in rice and onion; cover, reduce heat to low. Cook for about 20 minutes or until milk is absorbed and rice is done. Add tomatoes and cook on medium until juice has been absorbed. Stir in butter, salt and pepper. Serve hot.

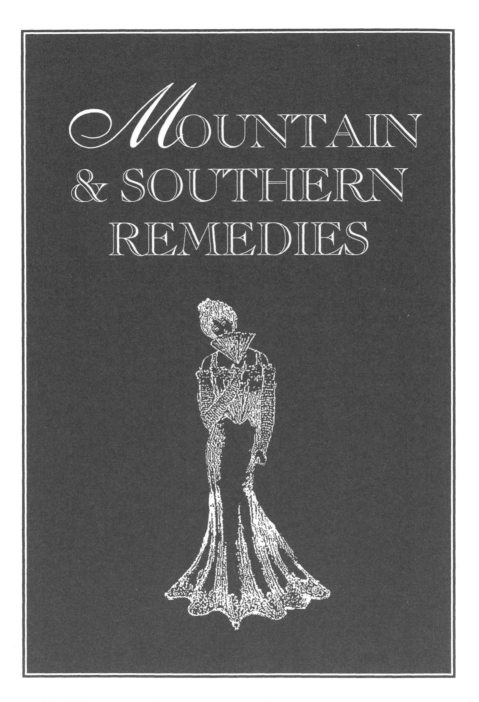

MOUNTAIN & SOUTHERN REMEDIES

CAUTION: The contents of Mountain and Southern Remedies are intended for your amusement only. We caution against any use of the remedies or cures. Even though these were used when we were children, there's no scientific proof documenting these to be safe.

CHILDHOOD MEMORIES

Remember as children all we had was each other,
Three little sisters and one dear brother.
We were poor, dirt poor, in our mountain home,
The four of us, Granny and Mama, our daddy
was gone. Deserted as children, looked down on
by others, such a heavy burden for our little shoulders.
We had to help each other and give a hand, as we fought
life's battles too young to understand.
Laughing and running over vine-covered hills, I close my
eyes, I go back, I can see us still. Going to bed hungry
didn't seem so bad, as we hugged together, Oh, what we
had. Love, friendship, acceptance too, knowing you would
look out for me, and I for you.
We're grown now yet our memories carry us back,
to the time before riches, furs and Cadillacs. To our home
in the mountains with the dirt floors, bad times, hardtack,
the creaking front door. Hard times and poverty on the
bound, but I'm thankful to God for what we found.
We still stand together as we did back then, standing
together through thick and thin. Feeling love and pride
when we look at each other, Three grown sisters, and one
dear brother.

POKE SALAD
(Poke Weed)

Poke weed is a springtime green that grows on a stalk. The flowers are greenish white, very poisonous, and should never be eaten. When mature, these turn to purple berries The leaves grow alternately along stalk. It is best to pick young leaves to make the salad. The salad requires that you wash the leaves thoroughly (like you would any fresh greens). When cleaned, place in a pot and bring to a rolling boil. Boil for a few minutes, then change the water. This must be done a total of five times. Season and cook until tender. If desired, you can place in a frying pan along with hot fat and scramble a couple of eggs in. Excellent with cracklin' cornbread.

Medical: We always ate poke salad at least twice a year. It was believed to purify the blood and guard against blood disorders.

RABBIT TOBACCO
(EVER LASTING LIFE)

Rabbit tobacco grows on a stalk. In the fall of the year, the leaves turn a brownish grey. When the leaves are stripped from the stalk, they can be boiled for tea. The tea is very bitter but it is said to be an excellent remedy for a chest cold. People have been known to smoke it, too.

SASSAFRAS

Sassafras tea was a delightful treat as a child. The flavor is very light and tastes very much like rootbeer. It is also used as a medicine.

To prepare the tea, the roots and bark were taken and cleaned thoroughly. A large pot was used to boil the two together until the tea became a rich, red color. Sassafras was said to be a narcotic in action and was given to girls to help alleviate menstrual cramps.

ONION

Onion is used in most mountain recipes and cures. A cough suppressant was made by simmering the onion along with honey or cane sugar to make a thick syrup. It was also tied to the bottoms of our feet to draw out the fever.

RAMPS

Ramps are a member of the wild onion family and are a very potent plant. They are cooked in recipes and also eaten raw. It is said the ramp helps to ward off a cold. If eaten raw, it will ward off more than a cold. It can be smelled on the breath for a week.

In our school days, it wasn't uncommon to see children sitting at their desks in the hallways during ramp season because no one could stand the odor.

This plant is a very important part of the mountain heritage. Every year there is a festival celebrating the season. The governor of the state has been known to attend.

CREASY GREENS

Creasy greens grow wild in the pastures, meadows and fields. They are ready to be eaten in the late fall and early winter. They are loaded with vitamins and were gathered not only for food but for this reason. Absolutely delicious with cracklin' corn bread.

Some grocery stores now sell creasy greens. They are located in the section along with the canned spinach and mustard greens.

BLACK WALNUTS

Black walnuts are a prized nut in the mountain regions and the southern flat lands. When the walnut falls from the tree, it is covered with a thick, green leathery outer shell. This will turn a dark brown when walnuts are ready to harvest, and usually takes a couple of months to dry out. It is best to wear gloves when removing the outer shell because it produces a yellow-brown stain that has to wear off. After the nut has dried, the shell is cracked open and the meat is picked out. These are used in candies, cakes, and ice cream.

PAW PAW

The paw paw is found on a tree that grows from 9' to 12' tall. It likes shaded areas and also grows along creeks. The fruit ripens after falling to the ground within a couple of days. When broke open, the pulp will be creamy and sweet. They are delicious eaten fresh or can be used to make desserts.

BLACKBERRY

Blackberries grow wild in the mountains and southern part of the country. They grow on vines with barbs (like a rose vine). In different regions, they are called by different names. In the mountains they are called blackberries. In the low country they are known as briar berries. By either name, they are delicious eaten fresh or in fruit pies, cobblers, or made into jellies and jams.

Medical: The juice was used to check acute diarrhea.

We remember as children picking blackberries for Sissy to can. We would take our little lard buckets (they were made of tin then) and pick all day. Our mouths would be purple and we would be as full of berries as our buckets by the end of the day.

Sissy would take what she needed, and we were allowed to sell the rest to the tourists that had summer homes in the mountains. We had our regulars that were happy to pay the fifteen to twenty-five cents per gallon for our berries. Even then it was the law of supply and demand. A bumper crop only brought fifteen cents, a lean year brought a whopping quarter!

We remember many days when supper was scratching at the ground at breakfast, and on a platter on the table for supper.

SUPERSTITIONS

MOUNTAIN SUPERSTITIONS

As children, we do believe our mom and grandma had a saying for everything. If you dreamed or did anything, it was a sure sign of things to come. And usually, the "things to come" weren't so pleasant. We truly know the meaning of living on the edge.

Naturally as children we "tempted fate." Needless to say nothing ever happened or we would have been gone along time ago.

We have compiled a list of the mountain and Southern superstitions for your amusement (and ours). We hope you have a good laugh!

• A whistling girl and a crowing hen always comes to the same bad end.

• If you hear an owl hoot at night, tie a knot in the bed sheet to ward off bad luck.

• If you lay your hat on the bed, back luck will come.

• If you hit someone with a broom, they will go to jail.

• If a bird flies in the house, there will be a death in the family.

• Don't wash on New Year's Day or you will wash away a member of your family before the next one.

• If you dream of fish, you will hear of someone being pregnant in the family.

• If you see the new moon with your hands in front of you, your troubles are ahead. If you see them with hands by your side, you're in the midst of trouble. If you see it with hands behind your back, your troubles are behind you.

• If you dream of snakes, you have enemies.

• Dreaming of a time peace is a sign of death in the family.

• If a black cat crosses the road in front of you, turn around and go another way or back luck will follow.

• Don't sweep under anyone's feet or they will never marry.

• If it rains on a bride, she will never be happy.

• If the right eye itches, you'll be mad. If it's the left eye, you'll be made pleased.

• If your right hand itches, you'll shake hands with a stranger. If it's your left hand, you will receive money.

• If you walk on crutches or ride in a wheel chair and don't need them, you will!

• If you hear a rooster crow at night, there will be a death in the family.

• If you forget something in your house and you've already gone out the door, don't go back in to get it unless you sit down for a couple of minutes or you will have bad luck.

• Place blue bottles in the window to ward off bad luck.

• If the bottom of your feet itch, you'll walk on strange ground.

• If you're walking with a friend or family member and come to a pole, both must walk around it on the same side or you will be separated in life. If you do walk on separate sides, you must say, "bread and butter," to prevent this from happening.

• If it thunders in January, there will be snow within twelve days.

- If it rains on a Saturday, it will rain seven Saturdays in a row.
- If you drop your dishcloth while cooking, company will come and they will be hungry.
- If you burn your bread, your husband is angry.
- If you're looking for someone to come, it is said, "a watched pot never boils."
- Don't take down the Christmas tree before New Year's Day or you will have bad luck all the coming year.
- Whatever you do on New Year's Day, you will do all year.
- There are certain days of the week to cut finger and toe nails. These are:
  - Cut them on Monday, cut them for health.
  - Cut them on Tuesday, cut them for wealth.
  - Cut them on Wednesday, cut them for news.
  - Cut them on Thursday, a pair of new shoes.
  - Cut them on Friday, cut them for sorrow.
  - Cut them on Saturday, see your true love tomorrow.
- Cut them on Sunday, your safety seek, the devil will have you the rest of the week!

According to Rose:
If you wake with a light heart, SING!!!

YA'LL COME!

My Friend

Concerned about my life, I walked in the
park on a warm summer morning.

A stranger approached me without
any warning.

He started a conversation with a how
do you do?

I said fine thanks, how about you'?

I then looked on his face there was a sweet smile

He said let's go sit on a bench and talk for a
while.

Something told me to go and I couldn't resist
I knew if I didn't there was something I'd miss.
He talked about life old and new.
He offered his opinion and asked, How about you?
How do you feel about your life and your past?
Have you made happy memories, one's that will last?
Or has there been pain and sorrow, things you'd like
to forget? I started to speak, He said no not yet.
I came to you because you're worried so,
I wanted to leave but I couldn't go. He said when you hurt, I hurt.
I'm not trying to be unkind, just learn from
your mistakes then leave them behind.
Hush now and listen and
I'm sure you'll learn, I'm not doing this out
of anger but love and concern.
As he turned slowly , with a wave of his hand, a
kaleidoscope of colors started spinning round.
I suddenly found my life being relived all over again.
It was like a good book I couldn't put down.

As I walked through my life, as I turned each page,

at times there was joy and other times rage.

I saw all the jealousies, the hurt and greed,

but I also saw kindness, and many good deeds.

Then I realized with startling clarity,

these are the things that make up this person called ME!

I felt a deep peace that comes from within, I then

turned to thank my new found friend.

But in His place I found a letter. It read:

My Precious Child,

I hope you're feeling better.

No one is perfect, I know you now see.

But you sat with perfection while you

sat here with me.

So take your troubles and throw them away.

It's time to start over, it's a new day.

And I know you think I've surely gone,

but I'm right here with you as I have been all along.

You've accepted me now and I've come in. It was simply signed

I love you,

Your Savior and Friend

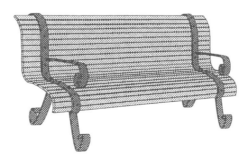

INDEX OF RECIPES

212

 CLOSING:
MY FRIEND

Published By
Rosemary Arrington Newman & Sharon Arrington Strickland

Sixteenth Printing